HITTING the Wall

FINDING PERSPECTIVE WHEN LIFE STOPS WORKING

DAVID S. PAYNE

HITTING THE WALL:
Finding Perspective When Life Stops Working
Copyright © 2010 by David S. Payne
First Printing - October, 2010
Second Printing - December, 2012

All rights reserved. Neither this publication nor any part of this publication may be reproduced or transmitted in any form or by any means, electronic or mechanical, including photocopying, recording or any information storage and retrieval system, without permission in writing from the author.

Unless otherwise indicated, all Scripture quotations are taken from the Holy Bible, New Living Translation, copyright © 1996, 2004, 2007 by Tyndale House Foundation. Used by permission of Tyndale House Publishers, Inc., Carol Stream, Illinois 60188. All rights reserved. • Scripture quotations marked (NASB) are taken from the NEW AMERICAN STANDARD BIBLE®, Copyright © 1960, 1962, 1963, 1968, 1971, 1972, 1973, 1975, 1977, 1995 by The Lockman Foundation. Used by permission.

ISBN: 978-1-77069-739-3

Printed in Canada

Word Alive Press
131 Cordite Road, Winnipeg, MB R3W 1S1
www.wordalivepress.ca

Library and Archives Canada Cataloguing in Publication

Payne, David, 1950-
Hitting the wall / David Payne.

ISBN 978-1-77069-739-3

1. Self-actualization (Psychology)--Religious aspects--Christianity. I. Title.

BV4598.2.P39 2012 248.4 C2012-905996-X

Table of Contents

Foreword

WALLS ARE DIVERSE. YOUR WALL MIGHT BE DISEASE, THE DEATH OF a spouse or parent, loss of a child, betrayal, joblessness, infertility, abuse, divorce, or some other challenge. You often don't see the wall until you hit it. But hit it, you do. And it always hurts.

When you hit the wall, you experience a sense of failure, hopelessness, despair. I know. I hit the wall of failed marriage and financial ruin. I was overwhelmed with loneliness, guilt, and shame. The amazing thing, however, was that as I came to the end of my own resources and efforts and discovered my hands empty, God met me with the tenderness of the Father for His prodigal son.

I worked hard at marriage, motherhood, and trying to make ends meet financially. All for naught. My marriage is over. My children go back and forth between households. And my financial situation is in disarray. But in my hopelessness and brokenness at the wall, God is renewing me and giving me His strength. My life hasn't changed dramatically, but I awaken every morning to God's love, tenderness, and ability to redeem. I have discovered hope and deep assurance in the midst.

The Scriptures reveal again and again that God wants each of us to come to the place where He is the epicentre of our being and existence. David Payne says it this way in *Hitting the Wall:*

> God will often allow you to hit the wall in order to bring you to the end of yourself. He allows you to arrive at the point

> of helplessness … You look in the mirror and come face to face with your frailty. It is at this point you begin to understand that the dream unfolding is God's dream and God's doing. You discover the presence and reality of God in a whole new way.

God takes men and women in their imperfection and pulls everything together for His own purposes. He uses the places of failure and defeat to bind us to Himself.

> Brokenness … is the place where you are spilled out. It lays open and bare the core of who you are. It is the place where you let go. But brokenness puts your heart in a better place. It is the place of surrender. It is the place where God picks you up. Where God begins to put you back together again. Where He begins to fill you with His favour, love, power, purity, joy, character, and life. Where He cultivates in you a deeper and richer relationship with Himself. It is the place where you find your life.

In *Hitting the Wall*, David Payne reveals his own personal wall experiences and brings to us the stories of others who have found themselves at life's walls. He also pulls from the stories of men and women in the Bible who hit their own walls and illustrates how God moved in their lives.

Think about King David who failed again and again. He didn't hide his failure. He did, however, always turn to the One who is able to save. The Father. As *Hitting the Wall* so aptly puts it:

> I've wondered why David, the psalmist and king of Israel, was called *"a man after [God's] heart"* (1 Samuel 13:14). It wasn't because he had a perfect heart. He didn't. He failed numerous times. But he had a tender heart that knew where to run when he failed. He would run to the Father and find forgiveness and refuge.

We also can run to the Father as baby chicks run to the shelter of the mother hen's wings. There we will find refuge and comfort. Forgiveness and protection.

> You are the evidence of what only God can do in a life at the wall, the place of pain, the place of brokenness, the place of surrender, the place of transformation.

God has a future and a hope for each of us. The promise is not for a life without pain or failure. It is, however, the promise of a life transformed—of brokenness restored.

—Amy Shelor
Editor

Introduction

Author Michael Lewis one day stumbled onto a story through his friendship with a man named Sean Tuohy. Lewis captured the story in a book titled *Blind Side: Evolution of a Game*. The story went on to become the motion picture *The Blind Side*. It is the story of a homeless, traumatized young man named Michael Oher who grew up to become one of the most coveted players in the NFL. How Michael began his life in the Memphis projects and what he became in life are miles apart. His mother was a drug addict. His father, whom he never knew, was murdered and thrown off an overpass. Michael possessed no birth certificate or any evidence he even existed. His life intersected with the Tuohy family more by divine intervention than anything else. With the help of this family—particularly Leigh Anne Tuohy, his adoptive mother—and his coaches, Michael made his way up the ranks to become an All-American offensive left tackle.

Michael's new life opened up a completely new world with incredible opportunities for him. The new environment, however, introduced numerous and equally extraordinary challenges. Obstacles. Walls. One of his greatest challenges was keeping up his grades in school. He had no experience or familiarity with the discipline needed to achieve academically. One night he expressed his bewildering feelings in an essay. It was an essay about walls.

> I look and I see white everywhere: White walls, white floors, and a lot of white people … The teachers do not know that I have no idea of anything they are talking about. I do not want to listen to anyone, especially the teachers. They are giving homework and expecting me to do the problems on my own. I have never done homework in my life. I go to the bathroom, look in the mirror, and say, "This is not Michael Oher." I want to get out of this place.[1]

Michael named his essay *White Walls*. We all encounter walls. If you think you haven't hit a real wall in your life, you will. Walls can be physical, emotional, or spiritual. They can be related to finances or failure. Shattered dreams. Betrayal. Abandonment. Infertility. Loneliness.

Walls often have a sense of loss associated with them. Loss of health. Loss of a loved one. Loss of employment. Loss of reputation. Loss of trust.

A wall is a barrier that rises up in front of you and threatens to block your way. Impede your progress. It is usually perceived as an adversary. Life stops functioning the way you want it to or are accustomed to it functioning. *Webster's Dictionary* defines a wall as "an extreme, desperate position. A state of defeat, failure or ruin."

A wall is something that can slowly build. Or it can rise suddenly. When the apostle Paul set sail from Crete into the Mediterranean Sea on his final voyage to Rome, a light, southerly wind was blowing. The conditions were perfect for sailing. *"But the weather changed abruptly, and a wind of typhoon strength (called a 'northeaster') burst across the island and blew us out to sea … so they gave up and let [the ship] run before the gale"* (Acts 27:14–15).

Can you identify? A south wind blew gently and warmly over your life. Life was good. And suddenly, everything changed. A cold wind of typhoon strength abruptly blew out of the north and drove you out to sea. You felt like giving up as you ran hopelessly before the gale. Today is so different from yesterday.

The following are the real names of people in my life who have hit the wall. All kinds of walls. Maybe you can identify with hitting one or more of these walls. Peter recently shared with me that when he was diagnosed with cancer three years ago, he treated it like a speed bump in his life. He believed God would get him past this like He had done many times with other things over his twenty years as a Christian. God did. Life seemed good again. Then just three months later, the dreaded cancer reappeared. This was not hitting a speed bump. This was more like hitting a stone wall at full speed. Peter's world did not slow down; it abruptly stopped. He described an overwhelming heaviness, a sense of helplessness and loneliness. All he and his wife could do was pray and cry; they did a lot of both.

Ross, a married father of three children, had just received a twenty-five-year award from his company for excellent service. One month later, on a Monday morning at 8:00 AM, he received a phone call from the company's vice president. Economics dictated Ross' termination. By 10:00 AM, the company computer, BlackBerry, and van were taken. Walls.

Tom excelled in all types of sports: baseball, basketball, hockey, football. He had dreams and aspirations of being a great athlete. A scholarship to university seemed achievable and imminent. That summer, while at a friend's cottage, Tom was climbing down a rock face and had a serious fall. He fell twenty feet, shattering his knee and cutting the main artery in his leg. He faced a fifty-percent chance of losing his leg. After many hours in surgery, his leg was saved. However, the injury brought an end to his sporting aspirations and career. Not only had Tom shattered his knee, he had shattered his dreams. Despair and dejection sucked him down into a lifestyle of partying, drugs, and alcohol. He attempted a comeback at football, but only three games into the season, broke his fibula and tibia and ended up in a cast up to his hip for six months. Tom hit the wall. It was an extremely low point in his life. Some years later, God got hold of Tom's life. Today, Tom recognizes that God had His hand on him all along, even through those very low points. In recent years, God has brought many people into his life. His injuries have helped him to relate to their pain, to encourage them, and to share his faith in Christ with them.

Ricardo left the doctor's office wearing the dreaded *C* word. He had come face to face with his mortality. For Scott, it was back surgery and facing the wall of a fifty-percent chance of never walking again. For

Marie, it was waiting at the wall of weight gain and struggling to lose another pound. For Mayra, it was watching her marriage disintegrate while doing everything she could to hold it together. For Suzanne, it was seeing her husband institutionalized with mental illness, and suffering at the wall of a long, lonely marriage. The illness took away a part of her husband she could not seem to get back. Walls.

Linda lay broken at the wall of an emotional breakdown. She had grown up in a pastor's home where she found herself as a child trying to live up to people's expectations and demands and learning to try to please everyone. When she grew older, she became busy in a demanding career. She found it difficult to say no. One day when she had nothing left in her, she collapsed emotionally. She was broken inside where no one could see the damage and pain. It was difficult for friends to understand. Recovery is taking a long time. Walls.

I prefer not to think of one person's wall as greater than or less than someone else's. How can we judge what someone else is going through? I prefer to simply think of walls as different. I have woven the true stories of people into the fabric of each chapter in this book. I begin each chapter with someone's story, a personal wall story. My purpose is to illustrate that walls are varied, but each is significant to the individual who hits it. I personally know each of the people who share their stories at the beginning of each chapter, and I know what God has done in their lives. For some of them, the recovery continues.

This book was spawned years ago. It springs from personal experience. I allude to two monumental walls in my own life. But I do not want this book to be one more story about failure, defeat, rejection, malice, hurt, and so on. I want to focus on hope, restorative grace, genuine recovery, and steady growth. I want the walls in my life to represent the walls in your life. And by sharing from my personal journey and the perspective I have discovered, I hope to help you find a biblical perspective at your wall and enable you to move beyond it.

God gives good news for the oppressed in Isaiah: *"To all who mourn in Israel, he will give a crown of beauty for ashes, a joyous blessing instead of mourning, festive praise instead of despair … They will be like great oaks that the LORD has planted for his own glory"* (Isaiah 61:3). In everything

God allows into your life, He desires to grow you into a strong fruit-bearing tree that brings Him glory.

During one of the turbulent times in my life. Carl, a very good friend, gave me a collection of songs. The words of one of those songs remain with me today.

> Under Your shadow I won't be afraid,
> Cover me, Lord, 'til the storm blows away.[2]

I learned what it means to be covered with the presence of Jesus. Some things become clear only in the storm. I wrote in my journal, "Father God, You have covered me with Your presence and carried me with Your grace. You have brought me a long way. Thank You."

I hope that by the time you finish *Hitting the Wall*, you will be able to journal the same thing.

This book was more recently born after I preached a series of messages on the same subject both in my own church and during a week of speaking at a summer conference. I was encouraged by numerous people to expand the material and put it into a book. One month following my time at the summer conference, I received an e-mail that sealed my decision to do so.

> This summer at Fair Havens Conference Centre, your message subject horrified me. I was afraid to attend. I wondered if I too would hit a wall. Well, today my husband of twenty-four years said, "It's too late. I love someone else." I am a good Christian. I have loved God and followed Him (past tense as of today). How could this happen to me? How will I survive? I hated your series, but I guess it was for me. No response required.
>
> —Susanne

Well, I did respond. More importantly, God responded. This was a marriage that crashed against the wall. But God specializes in putting pieces back together again. He is doing that in this marriage. He did it in my life. And He can do the same for you. Read on.

Beth's Story

I was a missionary, serving God away from home, doing what I knew God had called me to do.

I was home alone one night. My two young daughters were in bed, and, as darkness settled in, I was dozing on the sofa. Suddenly, I heard a noise. Enough of a noise to startle me. I realized someone was in the room. I felt frantic. I called out, "Who is it?" A man's voice answered, "Señorita." I froze. I could see the indistinct figure of a man coming toward me in the darkness. Immediately, the stranger was upon me, tearing at my clothes.

The strong smell of alcohol emanated from his breath. I screamed. Even though we were situated in a populated area, no one came. I struggled with the man and managed to get up into a sitting position. I lunged forward at him, sinking my teeth into his shoulder. He cried out in pain and threw me back onto the bed. He then fell from the bed, struggled to his feet, and staggered out of the room. Shaking, I ran to the room where my little daughters were sleeping and snatched them up in my arms. I then dashed to the bedroom, locked the door, and waited for my husband to arrive home.

I had many questions. We were serving God as missionaries away from home. We had already lost two children in death. Why that? And now, why this? Where was the Lord's protection? I allowed bitterness to take root in my heart. The bitterness crushed me emotionally to the point of considering suicide. Spiritually, I came to the point where I wouldn't read my Bible anymore. God's Word didn't seem to mean anything anyway. I couldn't pray. Why pray to a God who didn't seem to care what happened to me?

Then one day I had an irresistible urge to open my Bible. I opened it to 2 Corinthians 4:8–10. God had something for me that began to reorient my thinking and heart back to Him.

> *We are pressed on every side by troubles, but we are not crushed. We are perplexed, but not driven to despair. We are hunted down, but never abandoned by God. We get knocked down, but we are never destroyed. Through suffering, our bodies continue to share in the death of Jesus so that the life of Jesus may also be seen in our bodies.*

I never had been abandoned by God.

1 Authenticity at the Wall

PAIN. WHEN WE HIT THE WALL, WE FEEL IT. NONE OF US LIKE IT. WE try to avoid it, reduce it, erase it, even deny it. But there it is: a reality and absolute necessity for healthy existence. We would find ourselves in a desperate situation without pain. Pain warns of danger. It alerts us to something wrong in the body. It screams at us, *"Do something!"* It catapults the problem to the top of the brain's priority list.

Dr. Brand, who worked with leprosy patients for many years, wrote that leprosy patients suffer because they feel no pain.[1] Leprosy is a disease that destroys pain nerves, making the body extremely vulnerable to unimaginable injury. Can you imagine standing on a rusty nail without knowing it, or resting your hand on a hot stove without realizing it? Dr. Brand wrote, "At its most basic level pain serves as a signal that something is wrong, like a smoke alarm that goes off with a loud noise whenever the danger of fire reaches a certain level."[2] The absence of pain is like a destructive fire in a sleeping house without a fire alarm.

Pain serves a purpose. Pain is the greatest motivator to change. When you hit the wall, you know it because pain immediately informs you. The beginning of healing is to accept the reality of what has happened. The key to acceptance is authenticity in light of what has happened. Admit that this hurts. Acknowledge your pain. Come clean with your feelings. God gives you permission to do this.

WHY, LORD, WHY?

This lesson goes back to what is probably the earliest written book in the Bible. In a very short time, Job lost what seemed to be everything. He experienced the loss of his livestock, his business, his livelihood. He then suffered (an understatement) the tragic loss of his children in a devastating tornado. Finally, he experienced the debilitating loss of his health and dignity. God struck Job with a terrible case of boils from head to foot. He sat in a heap of ashes when his wife approached him and lashed out in her pain, telling Job to curse God and die.

She was a big help. Most pain hearkens back to a significant loss in your life. But rarely does one suffer the loss of so much as fast as Job did. And all for doing the right thing. Yes, sometimes you'll experience pain and loss for faithfully doing the will of God and remaining righteous. At first, no one knew what to say to Job. His friends just sat with him in silence, *"for they saw that his suffering was too great for words"* (Job 2:13).

How did Job respond? He cursed the day that he was born. *"Let the day of my birth be erased ... Let that day be turned to darkness. Let it be lost even to God on high"* (Job 3:3–4). It was night. The lights had gone out in his life and a heavy darkness overwhelmed him. His appetite evaporated as his greatest and oldest fears became a reality. He felt weary of the pain and longed to die. There was a depressing sense that God's compassion had deserted him and that he was destined by God to live in distress. Job saw no future. He felt "no peace, no quietness ... no rest" (3:26).

How did Job respond? He screamed out in pain. He shouted at God. Where was God? He struggled, doubted, wept, and confronted the situation with his true feelings. That is authenticity. When you feel the pain of the wall, God wants you to be honest and authentic with Him. He gives permission. It is a vital key to healing.

PAINFUL PRAISE

Actually, the majority of psalms are songs of complaint and inner struggle. As the psalmist cries out to God, we witness the tension between the pain of the wall and the presence of God. He tries to make sense out of the unresolved pain of hitting the wall against the backdrop of a God who is supposed to care but instead seems silent and uncaring.

Psalm 77 is an example of many such psalms. The psalmist begins, *"I cry out to God; yes, I shout."* He begins where we all need to begin: with authenticity. Laying your heart bare before God. Telling Him what you are feeling. God wants you to be honest with Him.

When was the last time you sang a song to God such as the psalmist sings in Psalm 77?

Gone again, gone again.
I've hit the wall, and You're gone again.
When I think of You, O God, I moan,
'Cause I've hit the wall, and You're gone again.
I'm overwhelmed with trying to find You.
I can't sleep; I can't pray;
Just thinking of the good old days.
O God, have You forgotten to be kind?
O God of neglect and insensitivity …
Who slams the door in my face!
It's obvious that You hate me …
hate me … hate me.
(author paraphrase)

You may feel uncomfortable with such perplexing frankness. But God gives you permission. That's authenticity.

THE BOOK OF WEEPING

When I think of authenticity, I think about a preacher called Jeremiah who did a lot of preaching but a lot more crying. That's why he is called the Weeping Prophet. He preached what God told him to say, that the nation of Judah must repent and return to God or else God would use the Babylonians as a tool to crush them. That was all well and good, except that now he was labeled a pro-Babylonian traitor and everyone held their noses and crossed the street when they saw him coming. But one day his enemies turned up the heat when they beat and bloodied him and then put him into the stocks (in Hebrew, the root word for *stock* means "to distort") at the north gate where everyone could get a good look at him. As people strolled by, they hissed and laughed at him, mocked him, and spat at him. When Jeremiah went home later that day, there were no joy bells ringing in his heart, no friends in his corner, and no converts to his preaching. He had been faithful to speak for God. But all for what? And where was God anyway?

Jeremiah had hit the wall. In Jeremiah 20:7–9, Jeremiah wrote that he felt like he had been lured into the darkness by Someone stronger than he was. He felt enticed and overpowered by God Himself. God had given him a passion to do something that made him a household joke. Jeremiah also cursed the day he had been born. He wished he had died in the womb. *"My entire life has been filled with trouble, sorrow, and shame"* (Jeremiah 20:18). This was not a good day to sing "Happy Birthday" to Jeremiah.

There is a book in the Bible named "The Book of Weeping." It is one long, sad funeral song. Guess who wrote it? Yes, you guessed it: Jeremiah. As he watched the Babylonians lay seige to the city, despair growing in the vacant eyes of the people, people dying of starvation in the streets, and mothers boiling the bodies of their own dead children to feed their remaining children, Jeremiah cried out in despair and also authenticity. *"[God] has led me into darkness, shutting out all light. He has turned his hand against me again and again, all day long"* (Lamentations 3:2–3). For Jeremiah, it was *night.*

> *He has broken my bones. He has besieged and surrounded me with anguish and distress. He has buried me in a dark place, like those long dead. He has walled me in, and I cannot escape. He has bound me in heavy chains. And though I cry and shout, he has shut out my prayers. He has blocked my way with a high stone wall* (Jeremiah 3:4–9).

Were there ever more distressing words written? Notice that Jeremiah says he has hit the wall and blames God for it.

I think many of us who call ourselves Christians are uncomfortable with expressing these kinds of feelings verbally to God. But we think them. We feel them. We simply block these powerful emotions from getting to the tongue because we think it is wrong to express doubts or anger or anything negative toward God. We want to be nice, respectable, and trusting—good Christians! But whether you express these sentiments in words or not, they are still there. I can remember feeling this way when I hit my wall. And then God reminded me, "You feel it. I already know it. It's okay to say it."

God wants you to feel secure enough with Him to be able to come to Him with honesty and authenticity. I remember the deep sense of freedom I felt when I was able to speak my mind with God. I was able to say it, He was able to handle it, and He still loved and accepted me. God's acceptance of you is grace-based. He wants you to be authentic with Him.

A REVELATION IN THE DESERT

One day after I had spoken to a group of people about authenticity, a woman came up to me in tears, thanking me for sharing these thoughts. To her they were both disturbing and freeing. As Liz's story unfolded, I found out she and her husband had hit a huge wall in their lives several years earlier. Their daughter Jennifer had been tragically killed in a car accident. It is hard to imagine the grief this can bring or the tension such a tragedy can cause in a marriage relationship. While Liz tried to hold to the party line of how she believed a Christian should respond, with faith and grace, her husband John responded quite differently. More like Jeremiah. "God has brought me into deep darkness. He has turned against me. Attacked me. Shut out my prayers. Blocked my path with a high stone wall!"

Liz admonished her husband for his unfaithful response. That didn't seem to help. She encouraged him to trust God. She warned him against questioning God and not accepting His will. The tension grew. The marriage faltered.

John had been a believer in Christ for more than forty years. He was a successful business owner, a loyal family man and husband, and an active member of his church. Nothing could have prepared him, however, for the journey he was to take. It began with that fateful phone call in October, 2001, that their youngest daughter had been killed. She had been driving leisurely along a street when a loud crash signaled an end to her life. John cried to God out of acute anguish. He shook his fist at God and angrily questioned, "Why did You let me teach my daughter to drive? Why did You let me convince her to go to Loyalist College … only to take her from me?" Could the darkness deepen? The next year, John's business failed. The strain between Liz and John was at the breaking point. Their thirty-year marriage was hanging by a thread.

To escape the pain, John got a job as a trucker and drove across country to the west coast. One night, he was returning on a stretch of highway that runs through the Mojave Desert. It had been a difficult day of driving in the rain and feeling that life was not worth living. Suddenly, all those powerful emotions of hurt and despair swelled and burst. He called out to God, actually screamed at God, "You could have saved Jennifer's life … but You didn't! You could have kept my business from failing … but You didn't! And You could stop this rain … but You won't! You could show Yourself to me … but You hide Yourself! You just want to punish me for all my sins and leave me alone on this road!"

At just that moment, John's rig broke the crest of a hill. He was stunned at what he saw. As he reached the crest, suddenly the sky opened up. The clouds parted. The rain stopped. Before him appeared the biggest full moon he had ever seen. It was as though God came to him, revealing His presence. The light of the moon pierced the darkness of the night while the light of God's presence pierced the darkness of John's soul. In the early hours of that morning, John pulled his rig to the side of the road and turned it off. He sat there for the longest time, just drinking in the silence of the desert and weeping bitterly. He was overwhelmed by the thought that just when he believed God had abandoned him, He showed His power over the heavens and came to him to quiet his aching soul. In the early hours of that morning in the Mojave Desert, John heard a still, small voice speak words of comfort and renewal to his spirit.

I still recall the morning Liz came to me and expressed her sense of disturbance and freedom at the thought of authenticity at the wall. Disturbance, because she was the one who had discouraged her husband from speaking his mind to God. She resonated with those identical feelings but had kept them buried within. He was the one who had been authentic with God in his struggle. Her admonishments and lack of support for his response had driven a wedge between them. She had been shackled by a lack of authenticity, a drive to perform in an outwardly acceptable way but not an honest way. She now felt a new freedom. She went to her husband and asked his forgiveness. She understood that it was okay to be open, honest, and real before God. It felt like the shackles had been broken and that she could relate to God in a new and authentic way. And she was free to join her husband in their journey together.

NIGHT

Elie Wiesel is a Jew who, as a young boy, survived the horrifying death camps of Auschwitz and Buchenwald. He witnessed the most shocking evil, including the death of his own family. Years later, he wrote a book called *Night*. It is one of the most moving, eye-opening books I have ever read. In this book he gives a heartrending account of the horrors he witnessed. He describes the day he was marched to the edge of a ditch from which leaped gigantic flames. He looked on as a truck delivered a load of little children to the flames. Elie's father began to whisper a prayer, "May God's name be blessed and magnified." Elie wrote, "For the first time, I felt revolt rise up in me. Why should I bless His name? The Eternal, Lord of the Universe, the All-Powerful and Terrible, was silent. What had I to thank Him for?"[3] One day he was forced to watch a young boy, like himself, hang and struggle at the end of a noose. Elie overheard someone ask, "Where is God?" Elie responded, "Where is He? Here He is—He is hanging here on this gallows."[4]

That day, as one child watched the hanging of another, Elie felt he had witnessed the death of God. "Where is the divine Mercy? Where is God? How can I believe, how could anyone believe, in this merciful God?"[5] Wiesel tries to resolve the horrors of the Holocaust with the idea of a sovereign and caring God. He asks good, legitimate questions that we all ask as we try to resolve the loving God we know with the sorrowful circumstances we encounter. Wiesel looks at human misery and treachery and sees the *absence* of God.

The Bible gives another perspective. In its pages we actually witness the torture, murder, and hanging of Jesus, God's Son, on a cross. We witness the death of God—for us. But then we witness the greatest miracle of all time, the resurrection of Jesus from the dead, offering life, forgiveness, and hope. The Bible looks at human misery and treachery and sees the *presence* of God.

One night, the prisoners in Elie's block held a mock trial. They put God on trial for the horrors of the Holocaust. Young Elie was called as a witness. In the end, God was found guilty of failing and abandoning His people, maybe even guilty of not existing. The mood was gloomy and dark. Have you ever experienced a time when the pain screamed so loudly and God seemed so silent?

THE ANCHOR OF HOPE

That's certainly how our weeping preacher Jeremiah felt. In Jeremiah 3:1–9, he lamented that all was night and that God seemed absent. He had hit a high stone wall, and God was nowhere to be found. And yet … and yet! As Jeremiah grieved over his awful loss, his despair suddenly took a turn in another direction. In the face of circumstance and feelings, he retreated to the refuge of truth. Jeremiah threw in the anchor. The anchor is called hope. *"The faithful love of the LORD never ends! His mercies never cease. Great is his faithfulness; his mercies begin afresh each morning … therefore, I will HOPE in him!"* (Lamentations 3:22–24, emphasis added).

What you have lost must not crush what you have. Hope points us in the direction of what we have. You are permitted and free to speak your mind with God at the wall, and it is healthy and safe to do so, because authenticity is anchored by hope in the character of God. Authenticity is not just ranting at God irreverently. It is evidence of one's security in the truth of God's unfailing love, and an affirmation of it.

At first glance, the word *hope* conjures in my mind an image of me drowning in a river, someone throwing a lifeline in my direction, and me hoping beyond hope that that rope is going to reach me. There is a chance it will. There is a chance it will miss. However, when the Bible speaks of hope, it is not referring to a hope-so sort of thing. Hope is a certainty. I know with certainty that the lifeline is going to find its mark, because I know the One throwing it.

Hope says … when things are out of my control, they are in His control.

Hope says … I can prepare for the worst, but expect the best. (It is this hope that fills the Air Canada Centre each fall when the Toronto Maple Leafs skate out onto the ice for another hockey season.)

Hope says … when it makes no sense to me, it makes sense to Him.

Hope says … when I feel alone, I am not alone.

Hope says … my pain is not in vain.

Many years ago, I read a colourful little booklet entitled, *Faith Is…* by Pamela Reeve.[6] Each page contained one succinct reflection about faith. Some of those thoughts still hang on the walls of my mind and can be interchanged with hope to serve as profound reminders of what hope is.

> Hope says … the Promiser keeps His promises.
>
> Hope recognizes … God is the "Master of time" when my idea of timing is out of sync with His.
>
> Hope is … confidence in God's faithfulness … in an uncertain world, … on an uncharted course, … through an unknown future.
>
> Hope is … depending on God's unending love and faithfulness and not on my ability to figure out why.
>
> Hope is … believing God has a purpose for my life and a plan for my good, when I feel everything about me is one big mistake.

When the nation of Judah was exiled into Babylon, just as Jeremiah the weeping preacher had warned, the exiles couldn't believe God had let it happen. They had hit the wall, and they were crying out to God to do something. They really thought God would recognize His big mistake and command an immediate reversal. So they didn't even unpack their suitcases. God told them, however, that they should unpack because this was no mistake and more than a vacation. This was a seventy-year sentence to be served inside Babylon. They were to settle down in their place of adversity. They were to accept what had happened and even make the best of it. Then God threw the anchor of hope.

God would not forget them. He had a purpose for their lives and a plan for their good. *"'For I know the plans I have for you,' says the LORD. 'They are plans for good and not for disaster, to give you a future and a HOPE'"* (Jeremiah 29:11, emphasis added).

Hope is the fuel for life. It lifts the eyes up and forward. It pierces the darkness. One of the most penetrating illustrations in the Bible of the bond between authenticity and hope surfaced at Jesus' crucifixion. It began in the Garden of Gethsemane, where Jesus was acutely shaken by the thought of His impending crucifixion. *"He became deeply troubled and distressed. He told them, 'My soul is crushed with grief to the point of death'"* (Mark 14:33–34). He went into a state of shock and asked the Father if there was not some way this cup of death could be removed from Him. These thoughts climaxed at the cross where Jesus, seemingly overwhelmed, cried out those despairing words, "*My God, my God, why have you abandoned me?*" (Mark 15:34). New Testament scholar William Lane describes the cry as, "ruthless authenticity … Jesus did not die renouncing God. Even in the inferno of abandonment he did not surrender his faith in God but expressed his anguished prayer in a cry of intimate affirmation, 'My God, my God.'"[7] Ruthless authenticity and intimate affirmation. Authenticity and hope in "My God."

A little while ago, a pastor's wife shared with me her sad story. She and her husband seemed to enjoy an unsinkable marriage. Then one day their Titanic hit an iceberg. They hit a wall they never saw coming. Her husband had a moral fall. When all had been publicly exposed and humiliation had set in, they were left with an aching sense of loss. Loss of ministry. Loss of income. Loss of church community, of home, of friends. Loss of everything, it seemed, in every aspect of life, except each other. They struggled with pain beyond words. They spent many hours crying out of the bitterness and despair of their souls to God. Amazingly, their marriage not only remained intact, but their commitment to each other remained strong. They had each other.

One day, one of the church elders sat down with her and expressed his sympathy regarding all that had transpired. He was the first of the leaders to actually sit down with her and show her any sympathy or concern. Her initial sense of encouragement, however, quickly changed to confusion and dismay. This man went on to express his regret that there was no hope for her husband to recover to the point of ever being in the centre of God's will again. God could not use him in any significant way. "No hope?" she asked. "No hope," he replied. He went on to ask her why she didn't leave her husband because of his sin and because, well, he could never be trusted again.

She looked up at me and smiled, and then added, "Since that time, God has blessed us with a strong pastoral ministry and an even stronger marriage."

Don't let anyone ever tell you that there is no hope. Whatever wall you hit, there is hope. The Bible tells you that death yields to resurrection.

Hope promises to turn misery to ministry. Mourning into joy.

Hope is the fuel for life's most despairing plights.

Hope is the fuel that restores passion back into life.

Hope is the fuel that stirs enthusiasm back into a marriage in its most desperate moments.

Hope is the fuel that burns within a parent, agonizing and persevering with a prodigal child.

Hope is the fuel that keeps a broken heart pumping.

Hope is why someone suffering from a life-debilitating disease can "speak life" into another human being.

Hope is the fuel that helps and motivates you to face today and then tomorrow.

The unfailing love of the Lord never ends! Great is His faithfulness. His mercies begin afresh each day. When you don't feel like getting out of bed in the morning, admit it honestly to God. Lay it all out there for Him. Then take hold of the anchor. Grasp the truth that His unfailing love greets you as your feet slip out of the sheets and hit the floor. It takes you by the hand and walks with you through the day. It tucks you into bed at night. And it greets you afresh all over again in the morning.

Ian's Story

I was a normal high school student. Sixteen years old. Life was good. I had just tried out for my driving license … and failed. My mother had come with me to the driver's test centre, and driving home I was less than happy. I told her so. As always, she was supportive and reassuring. I still felt miserable.

My parents had planned to leave that evening for a weekend at our family cabin. After dinner, my mother was cleaning up at the kitchen sink. My brother and I walked up on either side of her and gave her a big sandwich hug. She always liked that kind of thing. I was very close to my mother and my connection with her was affectionate and genuine. Before my parents left, I gave my mom a big hug, thanked her for taking time to come with me to the driving centre, and asked her to forgive me for being so irritable with her on the way home. Her forgiveness was always a given. She hugged me and said, "I love you."

The next morning I went to school … and my life changed. Everything I knew gave way. That evening I was at a church youth event. Oddly, my pastor called me to meet with him and my youth pastor outdoors. He asked us to come around to the side of the church building with him. I thought this was sort of peculiar. I asked him if everything was okay. His reply startled me.

"No, Ian, it's not."

We walked to the back of the building, and I asked again, "Is something wrong?"

"Yes," he replied, "very wrong." He seemed to be preparing me for something dreadful. I began to feel panicky inside. He asked me to sit down with him on the grass. Every emotion in my body was bracing itself. I could feel my whole being shaking.

He then said, "Ian, I need to tell you something that is going to change your life." Our eyes fastened. "Your mother has gone to be with Jesus." I froze. I felt paralyzed. He explained that she had been hiking in Algonquin Park and had tragically fallen from a cliff to her death. My emotions suddenly ruptured. The tears came. I cried uncontrollably for my mother. I sobbed until my whole body ached. The first thing out of my mouth was, "Did she feel any pain?"

"I don't know," my pastor replied.

It was in this place that I felt utterly alone. I knew God loved and cared for me, and that there were people in my life who loved me and would have done anything for me. But my mother had been my emotional, moral, and spiritual support. There had been no time to prepare for this. I missed her. There was an aching void for her. On the outside I tried to be strong, but on the inside I was broken. I didn't know how I was going to make it. It was like a bad dream where I was enveloped by an oppressive darkness. Suddenly, the ground had opened beneath me, and I was falling. I wanted to wake up but could not. For this was not a dream. It was my new reality.

2 Breaking at the Wall

IN THE WORDS OF THE FAMILIAR OLD NURSERY RHYME *HUMPTY Dumpty:*

> Humpty Dumpty sat on a wall,
> Humpty Dumpty had a great fall,
> All the king's horses and all the king's men,
> Couldn't put Humpty together again.

It is fun to sit on a wall. You can see all that is around. You feel the breeze blowing in your face. Life is good. You feel on top of your world. And then something happens. Tragedy strikes. Disappointment invades. Challenges overwhelm. Trust is broken. Dreams shatter. Failure lays siege to your life. You suddenly discover how fragile you really are. You try to hold on, but you begin to totter. Your shell cracks. You roll to the side and over you go, falling to the ground and breaking into a million fragments. You seem beyond repair. Friends and counsellors do their best to put you together again. And while they help, it seems to little avail. The wound is too deep. The break is too extensive. All the king's horses and all the king's men can't put you together again. The good news is that God can!

A DYSFUNCTIONAL HOME

A story begins in Genesis 37. It is one of the most interesting stories in the Bible. Joseph grew up in a family filled with jealousy and hostility. His father Jacob exacerbated the problem with the favouritism he showed toward Joseph. Joseph was the son of his father's favourite wife. Jacob sent his other sons to the fields to work while he sent Joseph to the store to buy candy. Joseph's eleven brothers wore hand-me-downs while Joseph was given a fashionable, brand-new robe with a note attached: "You're number one." Joseph's brothers hated him because it was obvious that their father loved him more than all of them.

Joseph grew up in a model dysfunctional home. This was a family waiting to implode. To make matters worse, Joseph dreamed two dreams. In the first dream, Joseph and his brothers were in the field tying up bundles of grain. Suddenly, Joseph's bundle stood up straight and the brothers' bundles all bowed down to his. In the second dream, Joseph saw the sun, moon, and eleven stars bow down to him. The dreams unmistakably portrayed Joseph as ruling over his family and their submission to him. If only Joseph had kept these dreams to himself, tucked away in his mind. But he couldn't. He had to talk. He flaunted the dreams in front of his brothers. He strutted his stuff. The second dream even irritated Jacob, who assumed that he was the sun. But the dreams ignited the furious rage of Joseph's brothers.

THE WALL OF BETRAYAL

One day, when Joseph was coming out to check up on his brothers in the fields, they recognized him approaching and saw this as their chance to dispose of him. They grabbed him, tore off his robe, and threw him into an empty cistern. Joseph fell with a thud onto the floor of the dry well. Stunned and confused, he gazed upward, the fine sand filtering down into his eyes. He tried to make sense out of what had just happened. The sky was blocked by the malicious faces of his brothers peering down at him. A couple of hours passed. The initial plan was to kill him. But when they heard a caravan of traders coming toward them, the brothers opted for plan B: to sell Joseph to the traders. "Instead of hurting him, let's reconsider. We don't want to be left with guilty consciences. After all, he is our brother. Let's be kind and sell him into slavery" (Genesis 37:26–27, author's paraphrase).

The brothers haggled for several minutes with the traders, arriving at an agreed price. Joseph was dragged up from his pit, shackled, and chained by the strangers to the harness of a camel. The tinkle of camel bells was set in motion once again as the caravan began to move. Joseph glanced back pleadingly but vainly into the empty eyes of his brothers. Terror and anguish gripped him. As Joseph made his grueling journey toward Egypt, walking in the dust of a camel, bound and naked, it became obvious that he had hit the wall! Betrayed by his own family. His trust broken. His dreams shattered.

THE WALL OF INJUSTICE

Could it get worse? Joseph was purchased by Potiphar, a very powerful and influential man, the captain of Pharoah's guard. At first, things seemed to go well. God was with Joseph and helped him to succeed in everything that he did (Genesis 39:2–4). But then one day, Potiphar's wife, who had become infatuated with Joseph, tried to seduce him. Joseph refused her attempts and tore himself away. The seductress was stung by the rejection and scorned Joseph, falsely accusing him of rape. Potiphar believed his wife and was furious. He had Joseph thrown into prison. Things had just gotten worse—a whole lot worse! Joseph now hit another wall, the wall of injustice. What chance did a slave have chained in a prison? He found himself on the same level as a sewer rat. Despised. Spurned. Disgraced. No rights for appeal. No friends for comfort. Broken. Alone.

Actually, Joseph was broken but not alone. God was with Joseph and made him a favourite with the prison warden (Genesis 39:21). Joseph had a way of becoming the favourite. Soon, Joseph was put in charge of the other prisoners. It's as though Joseph told himself, "I will not be a victim. If I am going to live on the level of a sewer rat, I will be the best, most productive sewer rat that ever lived. I will be the best prisoner in this dungeon."

GOD'S DREAM

I'm sure Joseph, like any of us, had dreams of his own. He most likely dreamed of owning his own herds and land, getting married and raising a family, living on the family ranch next to Dad's place. But his dreams had been shattered. He now lay broken against the wall of betrayal, injustice, disgrace. When his brothers hatched their diabolical plan, they commented, *"Then we'll see what becomes of his dreams!"* (Genesis 37:20). They thought their actions had shackled the dreamer and his dreams. However, there was something they hadn't taken into consideration. The dreams they referred to were not Joseph's—they were God's. There is one dream that will survive, and that is God's dream for your life. When Joseph was separated from his earthly father and crossed the border into Egypt, shackled, his heavenly Father crossed the border with him. God's dream was not fettered; it was unfolding.

As God's dream unfolds, He takes everything about you into account—family history, betrayal, injustice, failure, rejection, abuse, illness, shattered dreams, everything. Walls are part of the journey along which God leads you to the fulfillment of His dreams for your life. There are many examples in the Bible to illustrate this truth. Abraham and Sarah were promised by God that He would give them a son. The problem was that Abraham was already seventy-five years old and Sarah had just celebrated her sixty-fifth birthday.

But there was more. They hit the wall of infertility for another twenty-five years before Isaac was born. In those years of waiting, they tried to short-circuit God's dream only to reap the pain of splitting the family apart. When Isaac was finally born, it was obvious that he was a miracle baby. God had led Abraham and Sarah to the point where the outcome was something only God could do.

David, a shepherd lad, was anointed to be the next king of Israel. But before David became king, he found himself fleeing as a fugitive from the hands of a jealous and demented King Saul. David hit a thirteen-year-thick wall. And then he became the greatest king ever to rule Israel. The fulfillment of God's dream.

PAIN: THE GREATEST MOTIVATOR TO CHANGE

God will often allow you to hit the wall to bring you to the end of yourself. He lets you arrive at the point of helplessness. You are exposed.

He rips the mask off! You look in the mirror and come face to face with your frailty. It is at this point you begin to understand that the dream unfolding is God's dream and God's doing. You discover the presence and reality of God in a whole new way.

Warning! At that point, you are very vulnerable. You will go in one of three directions. You will allow your pain to paralyse and stagnate your life. Or you will allow your pain to drive you away from God and decide to move forward with your life as best you can without Him. Or you will say to God, "I cannot go on. From now on, it's You or nothing!" After the wall, you will never be the same. You will have a new normal. Your relationship with God will be changed. The wall becomes the door to transformation.

Hitting the wall is painful. But it is the pain that brings change. God had a dream for Joseph, a dream beyond Joseph's wildest imagination: he was to lead the world's most powerful nation out of crisis, and to save his own family and God's chosen family from starvation. But Joseph was an immature young man who flaunted favour, who spoke unwisely, who fanned the flames of jealousy and hostility, who seemed undiscerning, and who needed humbling. God had a dream for Joseph, but first, He needed to empty Joseph of Joseph. Joseph needed to hit rock bottom. God's plan would unfold through the process of pain and breaking. "God is wise enough to know that pain is the greatest motivator to change. It is a sad fact, but a true one."[1]

The Passion of the Christ, a film directed by Mel Gibson, parted the waters between those who acclaimed its excellence as a portrayal of the death of Christ and those who condemned it and Gibson for the film's graphic violence. After the film unsettled everyone who viewed it in one way or another, Gibson's personal life spiralled downward out of control as he relapsed into alcoholism. Personal strife and a disintegrating marriage after twenty-eight years opened him to such public humiliation that he withdrew from the screen, checked into rehab, and entered a self-imposed exile for eight years. He emerged from his period of separation with some keen insight.

John Hiscock conducted an interview with Gibson and wrote,

> It was when he began working on *The Passion of the Christ* that he says he "hit the wall," succumbing to the temptation of drugs, alcohol, and women until, he says, he reached "the height of spiritual bankruptcy … All of us have a point in our lives where we sort of hit the wall and it's very painful," he says. "As anyone knows, pain is always the precursor to change and it is no different in my case. I had got to a place of personal misery so it was time to stop and turn it back, and it was through faith and *The Passion,* which is the central theme of Christian faith, that I was able to come back."[2]

Whatever you think of Gibson and his many struggles, he came out of that time of exile with a profound, reflective discernment about the relationship between brokenness and change.

BROKENOLOGY

I call it the doctrine of brokenology—the study of brokenness. You read about it everywhere in the Bible. It was after David's sin of adultery with Bathsheba and the murder of her husband when David did what he did best. He wrote about it. He wrote, *"Purify me from my sins, and I will be clean; wash me, and I will be whiter than snow. Oh, give me back my joy again; you have BROKEN me—now let me rejoice"* (Psalm 51:7–8, emphasis added). And again, *"The sacrifice you desire is a BROKEN spirit. You will not reject a BROKEN and repentant heart, O God"* (51:17, emphasis added).

What is brokenness? More than five hundred years ago, St. John of the Cross penned a masterly poem and commentary called *Dark Night of the Soul.* He described the journey through brokenness with God as "purging the soul, annihilating it, emptying it or consuming in it (even as fire consumes the mouldiness and the rust of metal) all the affections and imperfect habits which it has contracted its whole life."[3]

Humpty Dumpty was an egg. An egg sitting on a wall may look fine, but a wall is a precarious place for an egg. It's an egg! Eggs break easily. The real essence of an egg is evident below the wall—when it's broken. We are more like eggs than we would want to admit. We can sit pretentiously on our walls, but we crack easily. We are fragile. Our real essence—our fragility—is more evident below the wall. When an egg breaks, it spills everywhere. God wants us to sit on the wall, for He has a dream for us that He is intent on fulfilling. But He must first break us. Spill us. Empty us. He must empty you of sin and of self and of all the stuff in your life that hinders God from filling you with His life and fulfilling His purpose and dream for your life. Stuff like pride, discontentment, greed, lust, impatience, envy, and shallowness. The list can go on and on.

You know you're feeling the pain of brokenness when you say, "God, if You don't come through for me, I'm not going to make it." Brokenness reduces you to the lowest common denominator. It's the place where you are spilled out. It exposes the core of your being. It is the place where you let go. But brokenness puts your heart in a better place. It is also the place of surrender, and the place where God picks you up. Where God begins to put you back together again. Where He begins to fill you with His favour, love, power, purity, joy, character, and life. Where He cultivates in you a deeper and richer relationship with Himself. It is the place where you find your life.

WALKING WITH A LIMP

I remember, not long after my time of brokenness, when I was still healing, that I needed someone to talk to. It's hard to find someone you think will understand. I heard Gordon MacDonald was going to be in our city for a series of preaching engagements. Gordon had experienced failure and brokenness in his own life. He had written a book titled *Rebuilding Your Broken World*, and so I thought, "Here would be someone to talk with."

I contacted Gordon, and we arranged a time to meet. We planned to connect for breakfast but ended up spending the whole morning together. We shared our stories and talked about brokenness and healing, and he said something that has always stuck with me. "You will always walk with a limp after God has broken you, like Jacob, but let that limp be a reminder not of your weakness or failure, but of what God has done in your life through breaking you."

THE "GRACE" GARBAGE TRUCK

I need to say that there is one thing that will really mess with God's dream for your life. One wall against which you can break and do a lot of damage to the course of your life. That wall is sinful disobedience. Sin is the great wall that comes between you and God, between you and God's dream for your life. The good news is God has even taken that into account. *"Where sin increased, grace abounded all the more"* (Romans 5:20 NASB). Where sin abounds, grace superabounds. God has provided everything you need to turn around. Jesus died for all of your sin and guilt. He has paid the penalty and the price for your sin by giving His own life. Now what you must do is confess and forsake your sin. *"But if we confess our sins to him, he is faithful and just to forgive us our sins and to cleanse us from all wickedness"* (1 John 1:9).

Confession means "to say the same thing" as God does about your sin. "God, this is what my sin is. This is what You call it. This is how it hurts You and how it has hurt me. I understand what it cost You to forgive me." Confession means to get your sin out to the curb. You need to go through every room in your life, especially the basement of your desires, motives, and thoughts. Pick up all the sin and garbage you can find and get it out to the curb. Every day, a large garbage truck drives up to the curb of your life. On the side of the truck is the word *GRACE* painted in big red letters. Jesus is the garbage man. His hands and feet are bleeding from His work. But He always seems to have a smile on His face and love in His eyes. He stops at the curb where my garbage is sitting. He jumps out of the cab, strolls around to the side of the vehicle, picks up the garbage, and hurls it into the huge, gaping mouth at the rear of the container. He then drives away with it. The sound of the truck grows faint in the distance. I don't know where He takes it, but I never see it again.

Sin need never stand in the way of God's dream for your life. Christ's death has provided for sin's removal. His resurrection has broken sin's control. Check out Romans 6. God's grace is greater than every sin. This means brokenness can lead to full restoration of God's dream for your life. God's grace will restore you to either the same dream, a revised form of the same dream, or a new dream. If grace is greater than all sin, then God restores fully. You do not need to accept what some people call God's "second best." There may be and often are consequences that endure, but you can live in the centre of God's dream and enjoy full restoration. J. I. Packer wrote,

> It is the same when a Christian wakes up to the fact that he has missed God's guidance and taken the wrong way. Is the damage irrevocable? Must he now be put off course for life? Thank God, no. Our God is a God who not merely restores, but takes up our mistakes and follies into His plan for us and brings good out of them. This is part of the wonder of His gracious sovereignty. "I will restore to you the years that the locust has eaten … you will have plenty to eat, until you are full, and you will praise the name of the Lord your God, who has worked wonders for you" (Joel 2:25, 26) … Slippings, and strayings there will be, no doubt, but the everlasting arms are beneath us; we shall be caught, rescued, restored. This is God's promise; this is how good He is.[4]

Before I leave the subject of brokenness and restoration, I'd like to explore it a little further in the life of another man who fell from the wall and look at what happened next.

Alexis' Story

I HAD HEARD THAT DIVORCE WAS ONE OF THE MOST PAINFUL WALLS ONE can hit. I just never thought it would happen to me. It did.

In looking back on that experience, my life was caught up in a "dust storm." My whole life was mired in a whirlwind of words I had thought I would never have to deal with. Words like "separation agreement," "lawyers," "in specie," "audits," "custody," "child support," "spousal support," and "decree."

My secure and stable life as I had known it was over. Looking ahead was truly terrifying for me. I was forced to start life over again and find a new place to live, a new job, new friends, and ultimately peace.

People who had been through this ordeal before told me that life would be okay and that I would settle down to a "new normal." I shook my head at this in disbelief. How could life be "normal" when everything had changed?

I felt a strong sense of fear of the unknown, of being by myself, of having to ultimately support myself. I felt anger and frustration—towards my to-be ex-spouse, and towards God. I knew God was there helping me through everything, and I honestly don't know how I would have endured without Him. But I was still angry at Him. Why was this happening? I argued, "If divorce is not Your will, why don't You fix this?" I had a deep, pervasive feeling of emptiness and sadness that persisted with me for about two years. I lived, breathed, and slept with this crisis, consumed by it. I felt trapped in a dust storm that would not settle and overwhelmed by emotional pain that would not end. I experienced deep grief, mourning the loss of my marriage, my stable and secure life, my family and my home.

Ultimately, I was enveloped by an all-encompassing sense of guilt. Guilt for the responsibility that I held for what was happening. This was what hurt the most. The guilt became even more crushing whenever I thought of my children going through this upheaval in their young lives and being brought up in a "broken" family. It was agonizing to think of possible irrevocable damage to them and that my youngest would never know how it felt to have an intact family.

It's amazing to realize that after the passing of years, some of these emotions remain close to the surface, closer than I realized. And they can be extracted with little provocation.

3 Failure at the Wall

DIANE AND I WERE ON VACATION. WE WERE WALKING IN THE SAND along the ocean, watching the waves breaking as they approached the shore. Our goal was the pier, just the right distance for an evening stroll. The smell of fish saturated the air, and the squawking of seagulls reached a shrill as they attacked the entrails of a fisherman's catch just scraped off the cleaning table and into the water. As we walked out onto the aged, wooden pier, we noticed a young man sitting at a picnic table with an open Bible before him. He was oblivious to our presence for he had his head bowed and seemed very intent in prayer. I wished I could engage him in a conversation, but did not want to interrupt what God might be saying to this young man.

We walked to the end of the pier and were peering out into the endless horizon when the young man was suddenly standing beside us. A voice seemed to say to me, "Go speak to him." I moved over beside him and commented that we had noted him at the other end of the pier. I introduced myself to him, identified myself as a Christian, and wondered if he needed someone to talk to. He looked at me rather stunned. I immediately wondered if I had stepped into something that was none of my business.

After a brief but uneasy silence, he opened his mouth and introduced himself: "I'm Jody, and my life is a mess." He explained that he had surrendered his life to Jesus just a year earlier, but that he was such a failure. When he'd gotten home from work that night, he could feel himself emotionally spiraling downward. He continued, "I have let God down, my best friend down, and myself. I hate myself, and I feel no reason to live on." He told us that as these destructive thoughts persisted, a voice seemed to be telling him to go to the pier. He wasn't sure why, but he picked up his Bible and went anyway. "I sat down at a table, read my Bible for a few minutes, and prayed for God to say something to me. I waited. Then I heard that same voice urging me, 'Go to the end of the pier for ten minutes.' I thought that kind of strange, but here I am."

That was when our paths intersected. God's timing is perfect. Jody didn't tell me what his failure was. I didn't ask. But I knew it was something that had rocked his life and had shattered his confidence. I knew a pattern of failure had reinforced his sense of hopelessness. I tried to speak into his life, to let him know that failure described what he had done but did not define who he was. I reassured him that nothing is hopeless when it comes to what God is doing in our lives. I reminded him that simply thinking about how our paths had intersected was evidence of how God had not given up on him. He still seemed astonished with what had just happened. He kept repeating, "I just can't believe it; I just can't believe it!" I looked at my watch. Our conversation had been ten minutes. I reminded him that God had allotted ten minutes and that I wouldn't want to stand in the way of God's directions. He shook hands with me, thanked me for stepping up and speaking with him, and we separated ways.

The wall of failure is a reality in life. God has filled His book with many people who broke against that wall. Meet Jacob. Moses. David. John Mark. The list could go on and on.

Who can forget Jonah? God commanded Jonah to go one way, and Jonah bought a one-way ticket going the opposite direction. But that wasn't the end of it. God pursued him. Read the first chapter of the book of Jonah. God prepared a violent storm and arranged for a great fish to swallow Jonah. The fish held Jonah for three days, when it finally threw him up onto the beach (Jonah 2). Jonah lay there on the beach, facedown in a whale-load of barf, and then realized that he *was* the barf. A failure! For sure! Even the fish didn't want him. But then you read,

"Then the LORD spoke to Jonah a second time" (Jonah 3:1). I love that verse. No matter how you have failed, God is the God of a second chance.

FAILURE, BIG TIME!

The failure that has most impacted my life was committed by one of Jesus' disciples. Peter walked right beside Jesus. He heard everything Jesus said and saw everything He did. He walked in the dust of the Rabbi. Like Joseph, God had a dream for Peter. Peter seemed like the right guy for God to use. He was the one who was quick to affirm his loyalty to Jesus. He confidently informed Jesus, *"Lord, I am ready to go to prison with you, and even to die with you"* (Luke 22:33). The problem was that while Peter bristled with self-confidence, he was blind to spiritual reality. I think that his intentions were good, but he misunderstood the weakness of the flesh and the power of the enemy, the devil.

Jesus opened the shade just a little for Peter to look through. He looked directly at Simon Peter and warned, *"Simon, Simon, Satan has asked to sift each of you like wheat"* (Luke 22:31). While Satan would have liked to destroy each of Jesus' disciples, Peter was in the direct line of fire. Peter was in the battle of his life and for his life. Satan wanted to completely obliterate Peter. The source of spiritual failure is our human fleshly weakness when it is manipulated or exploited by a spiritual power stronger than we are. Jesus warned Peter that there was a dragon waiting to swallow him. Peter thought he was ready for battle, for he was more confident than his fellow disciples and his sword was at his side (Luke 22:38).

Jesus continued, *"But I have pleaded in prayer for you, Simon, that your faith should not fail"* (Luke 22:32). Isn't it wonderful to know that Jesus prays for us? It was this same final week that Jesus prayed, *"Father … my prayer is not for the world, but for those you have given me, because they belong to you … I'm not asking you to take them out of the world, but to keep them safe from the evil one"* (John 17:1, 9, 15). Peter's faith would fail, but *not* completely. Even when we are in over our heads and foolishly fail to recognize it, Jesus rescues us. We fail to take hold of the spiritual weapon of prayer, but He takes hold of it and wields it. Because of Him, failure need never be final.

In fact, failure can become the beginning of a new day. Jesus was about to die upon a cross for people like Peter. Sinners. Failures. He was about to go to a cross so that sinners need never be completely swallowed by sin, nor failures by irreversible failure. He would die to give hope. Jesus looked ahead and laid out a pathway of recovery. *"So when you have repented and turned to me again, strengthen and build up your brothers"* (Luke 22:32). The Master of Restoration says that when you repent, and repentance is the key to restoration, He will restore you from your misery to ministry, from failure to fruitfulness. He will restore you to the point where you can use your example of pain and failure to encourage and build up others who are failing in the struggle.

With this warning and word of hope, Jesus and His disciples walked out into the night. And it was about to get a whole lot blacker, more acute and dreadful than Peter ever imagined. Jesus was arrested, beaten, mocked. And Peter deserted Him, stayed far behind Him, and failed Him. Not once, not twice, but three times. Three times someone approached Peter and asked him if he was one of Jesus' followers and three times Peter denied it. So much for, *"You can count on me, Lord."* So much for loyalty. So much for courage.

BITTER TEARS

And then come some of the most somber words in the Bible: *"At that moment the Lord turned and looked at Peter"* (Luke 22:61). What a look! But not a look of surprise, for Jesus knew already that Peter would fail under the pressure. Not a look of condemnation, for Jesus was about to take upon Himself the condemnation of Peter. Not a look of rejection, for Jesus was about to be rejected for Peter as proof that He accepted him and loved him beyond anything and everything. Not a look of futility, because Jesus had already laid out the hope of recovery.

It was a look of knowing, a look that broke Peter's heart. The grief, hurt, disappointment, and pain over what had just happened overwhelmed him. The pain of failure was excruciating. As their eyes locked, Peter jumped up from the warmth of the fireside and ran out of the courtyard into the cold street, weeping bitterly.

The pain of failure is crushing. So crushing that it can break the heart. It can elicit some of the bitterest tears you will ever cry. I clearly remember the bitter tears I cried after I had hit my wall of failure. I blamed myself. I felt I needed to punish myself. I felt I had so disappointed, hurt, and failed my family that I didn't know what to do but to weep. At night, when Diane was sleeping, I would stand over her and weep. "What a failure I was. She was not deserving of this. I was not worthy of her. I was a horrible husband." And the tears would stream down. Then I would go into my young son's bedroom and weep. He was everything to me. I would torment myself. "What an awful father I am. Does he know how much I have failed him?" I felt acute anguish as I entered the bedroom of my two small daughters. I would look down into their innocent faces and listen to their breathing, and the tears would flow like a river. How could I ever make things up to them? I followed this torturous routine for many nights.

Strangely, I was feeling a peculiar connection with God. Something in my nature was changing. I was learning that at no time are you closer to God than when your heart is breaking. The brokenness of failure is closely connected to the brokenness of Jesus' body and the brokenness of God's heart. My heart was spilling and feeling cleaner than it ever had. I was being more authentic with God and about myself than I had ever been before. Even though I was experiencing an acute sense of alienation and rejection from church, friends, and fellow pastors, I was feeling forgiveness from God. I could feel His strong arms around me and the touch of the Master's hand beginning a work of healing and restoration.

Our marriage was strong. Diane was a rock and held on to me when emotionally I was dropping. One day I received a note from her. She wrote, "Being married to you is the best thing that ever happened to me." She knew just how to lift me and give me hope. There were a few friends who stood by us, encouraging and supporting. One day a friend handed me a note with a Scripture verse written out.

He is able to do …
able to do exceeding …

able to do exceeding abundantly …
able to do exceeding abundantly beyond all … that we ask or think.
(Ephesians 3:20, NASB)

The Holy Spirit focused my mind and heart on the psalms, especially the first fifty psalms. The sentiments of the psalmist were mine, and I prayed these prayers to God. In these scriptures I found huge comfort, assurance, and release.

God directed my attention to two books that really helped to reorient my thinking and give hope. *Failure: The Back Door to Success* was a title that seemed to fly in the face of general sentiment within the context of Christian culture. The title got my attention. Erwin Lutzer wrote, "This book is written for those who believe they are failures and for those who falsely believe they aren't! It is a message of hope to those who are filled with regret; it is a message designed to disturb those who mistakenly feel they have 'made it' in life."[1] I read on.

The second book was by Dean Merrill, *Another Chance: How God Overrides Our Big Mistakes*. This title also captured me. Merrill wrote, "It's okay to run to the Father. In fact, it's the smartest thing you can do at the moment. It is your one route to freedom from the confusion, guilt, shame, and self-doubt that hammer at your sanity."[2] Well, running to the Father was what I was doing. I felt His welcoming arms. He truly is the God of a second chance. I've wondered why David, the psalmist and king of Israel, was called *"a man after [God's] heart"* (1 Samuel 13:14). It wasn't because he had a perfect heart. He didn't. He failed numerous times. But he had a tender heart that knew where to run when he failed. He would run to the Father and find forgiveness and refuge.

ANOTHER CHANCE

And then, again, there was Peter. Repentance, or turning around, is the key to restoration. If one does not repent, restoration is not possible. But Peter had wept bitter tears of repentance. Jesus had told him that repentance and turning to Christ again comprised the path to restoration. However, the pain of failure had caused too much injury and loss. Perhaps the obstacle for Peter was skepticism that Christ could ever use him again in His kingdom work because of what he had done. How could Jesus ever trust him again? Perhaps it stemmed from self-condemnation and a lack of self-forgiveness. At any rate, Peter decided it would be easier to turn back at the wall. So he returned to his old fishing career.

The inability to forgive oneself is a huge obstacle and will shackle your spiritual progress. I know that was true for me. You feel you have hurt God and others so much, and you feel such a great degree of disappointment in yourself and self-condemnation that self-forgiveness eludes you. You believe God has forgiven you, but how can you forgive yourself? Something Dean Merrill wrote opened my eyes. "Are you holier than God is? ... Must God sacrifice another Son just for the sake of your conscience? ... If the death of Christ was good enough for God, isn't it good enough for you?"[3] The dawn began to break.

But even when you have experienced forgiveness, can God pick you up out of the ashes of failure and use you to the same extent again? Yes, He can, if His grace is greater than anything. Can He fully restore a person who has hit the wall of failure? Absolutely, if you understand what happened next in the life of Peter. Something Peter hadn't counted on. Jesus pursued him!

You need, first of all, to have an understanding of grace. Grace is foundational to forgiveness and restoration. Grace eclipsed everything at Calvary. When Jesus died on the cross, God's grace merged with His justice. Jesus paid the price that God's justice demanded for sin. Your sin. Grace says you need not punish yourself for what you have done; Jesus was punished for you. You don't need to satisfy God; Jesus did that. You don't have to pay for your sins; Jesus paid it all! That's grace. No sin is too great. No sinner is too fallen. No failure is too shameful. Jesus said, *"I tell you the truth, those who listen to my message and believe in God who sent me have eternal life. They will never be condemned for their sins, but they have already passed from death into life"* (John 5:24).

Lutzer gave an illustration of the early Canadian pioneers facing down a prairie fire that threatened to devastate everything in its path. The one way of escape was to build a counter fire. They would begin a fire right where they were, fanning the flames outward from their dwellings toward the larger raging flames leaping nearer. They would then stand together in the place where the counter fire had already burned. They rested secure that the flames can't get you when you are standing where the fire has already been.[4] Grace says that when you stand by faith on the ground where Jesus endured the wrath and justice of God against your sin for you, you are safe.

Grace is the reason for your eternal salvation. But grace is available and applied to your life daily. You don't understand grace until it's all you've got. But when grace is all you've got, it is enough. God's grace meets you in the area of your greatest need. It is adequate to turn any situation into good. When you fail, His grace meets you there.

BREAKFAST AND A NEW DAY!

Jesus knew Peter's heart. And it was Peter's heart and Jesus' extravagant restorative grace that drew Jesus to Galilee's shores that morning. Jesus pursued Peter. Have you ever been pursued by God? Peter had been fishing all night with some of his fishing buddies. They had caught nothing. It seemed that no vocation was working out for Peter. Jesus knew where to find him. The Capernaum fishing grounds were just down the road from the village of Capernaum. The warm water from the hot springs in the hills above flowed down into the lake at this spot, warming the lake water a few degrees. The fish would congregate here, and so would the fishermen. It is one of my favourite spots.

This is also one of my favourite stories, found right at the end of John's Gospel in chapter 21. The stranger on the shore called out and instructed the weary, unproductive fishermen to throw their nets on the other side of the boat and they'd find plenty of fish. They obeyed, and the nets immediately filled. The disciple John, also in the fishing boat, was the first to put two and two together. As they strained at the nets, the scene evoked in his mind something that had occurred three years earlier, something so similar that the likeness was too obvious to question. Jesus had given an almost identical command and the results had been the same (See Luke 5:4–11). Both John and Peter had been so amazed that they had responded by leaving everything and following Jesus.

John cried out, *"It's the Lord!"* (John 21:7). When Peter heard this, he reacted in typical "Peter" fashion. Peter's repressed, emotional sense of failure and shame exploded, and he hit the water like a cannonball and swam to the shore. When he arrived, Jesus already had breakfast frying over a small fire. Fresh fish and bread. I can picture the scene so clearly. The smell of fish frying. The sound of sizzling fat in the frying pan interrupted only by the gentle rippling waves washing the pebbles on the shore. A low mist hung over the lake. The cool morning air lingered, and the fishermen huddled close to the fire to cast off its chill. The sun's first rays were just beginning to rise over the steep hills on the eastern shore of the Sea of Galilee, casting their early glow over the water and illuminating the shore as they stretched westward.

It was a sacred moment. As breakfast came to an end, those same eyes that had pierced Peter's heart as he warmed himself by the courtyard fire just a few nights ago were searching for him again. Peter tried to keep his eyes trained down. But in just one unguarded second, as he lifted his head in the direction of the charcoal fire, his eyes locked with those of the Saviour. Another fire. Same eyes. Compassionate, tender, searching. Like the eyes of a Shepherd looking for His wounded, wayward sheep.

Jesus got up and beckoned to Peter with His hand. They strolled along the shore. After they had gone just a short way, Jesus stopped. He looked again at Peter with those penetrating eyes and asked, "Do you love me?" (John 21:15, paraphrase). Peter was adamant that he did. It took a few tense moments to affirm this, and then it was as though Jesus wanted to know, then, why Peter was fishing when Jesus had called him to feed His sheep. Jesus had returned to Galilee to restore Peter to what He had originally called him. He had just died and risen from the dead for people like His wounded disciple.

Extravagant grace + repentance = full restoration. A formula that always works. For anyone. For any sin or failure. Because Jesus' blood and life stand behind it. Peter would be the first to experience the full restoration Jesus had come to provide. The first to receive the gospel of a second chance.

Jesus then informed Peter that if he followed Him, it would cost him his life. If Jesus shared that kind of information with you, would you follow Him? Peter did. He did not disappoint Jesus. He was so impacted by the gospel of a second chance that he never looked back. It is interesting to note that God used Peter much more after his failure than He ever did before. On the day of Pentecost, it was Peter who rose to preach, and three thousand responded to the good news. When the church was born, it was Peter who led the charge. History tells us Peter was crucified upside down because he would not deny the Lord. I don't think Peter ever forgot that morning on the shore of Galilee. It was never far from his mind that he was living proof of the power of the restorative grace of God to transform a human life. Broken. Restored. Surrendered.

I've said a lot in this chapter about grace. *Grace* means "gift." However you cut it, grace is an amazing gift. It is the reason for Jesus' cross. It overcomes evil. It meets any need. It is stronger than any failure. It is irrational. It gives hope. It always gives another chance. It is the pathway to healing. It is the gift that keeps on giving.

THE EMBRACE OF GRACE

Nelson Mandela endured twenty-seven years in prison. His story is one with surprising parallels to the biblical story of Joseph. Both men endured many years unjustly in prison. Both men emerged from prison to become great, influential leaders: Joseph, to become second only to Pharoah; Mandela, to become president of South Africa. Both leaders were given the power and opportunity to take revenge on those who had committed such evil and injustice against them. Both men chose not to. Instead, both men chose healing over justice, forgiveness over punishment, restoration over revenge. Joseph spoke kindly to his brothers, who had so brutally betrayed him, and assured them of his forgiveness. He reassured them that he would take care of them and their families (Genesis 50:21).

In similar fashion, Mandela appointed Archbishop Desmond Tutu to lead something called the South African Commission for Truth and Reconciliation. This commission was designed to divert a vengeful, violent bloodbath between blacks and whites, victims and oppressors, after years of injustice. The plan and purpose was to hear both sides.

Victims were invited to come forward and tell their stories of abuse. Oppressors were also invited to voluntarily come forward, tell the truth about what they had done, admit their guilt for their crimes and inhumanity, and ask for amnesty.

In one courtroom, an elderly black woman listened to white police officers give account of their atrocities. One man, officer van de Broek, looked at the woman and acknowledged how he and some others had shot her eighteen-year-old son and partied while they burned his body, turning it over and over in the fire until nothing remained. He recounted how eight years later, he and others returned to arrest her husband. They forced her to watch as they tied him to a woodpile, poured gasoline over him, and ignited him. His last words were, "Forgive them." Now van de Broek asked forgiveness and awaited the judgment of the court.

The elderly woman was asked by the commission to respond. She did. The room was still.

"I want three things," she said. "I want Mr. van de Broek to take me to the place where they burned my husband's body. I would like to gather up the dust and give him a decent burial.

"Second, Mr. van de Broek took all my family away from me, and I still have a lot of love to give. Twice a month, I would like for him to come to the ghetto and spend a day with me so I can be a mother to him.

"Third, I would like Mr. van de Broek to know that he is forgiven by God, and that I forgive him, too. I would like to embrace him so he can know my forgiveness is real."

As the elderly woman was led across the room to give her embrace, van de Broek fainted, overwhelmed. From the corner, someone began to sing *Amazing Grace*. More voices joined in, and soon everyone was singing.[5]

Grace is always amazing. It doesn't just say, "I forgive you, but..." It goes the extra step to restoration. The elderly woman forgave. But she did more. She responded to her abuser's repentance and embraced him, asking him to allow her to care for him as a mother. That's restoration.

You may be damaged goods. But the cross is proof of the extent to which God will go to restore you to Himself. Whatever you have done, however you have failed, Christ stands with open arms, ready and wanting to embrace you. He longs to care for you as a loving and forgiving Father. He desires more than anything to heal and restore you. Like restored furniture, the scars add to your beauty and value. They are the record of wounds and tell a story of the workmanship of the Master Restorer in your life. He desires to take you by the hand and lead you forward. And, believe me, you will never be the same again after being touched by His amazing grace.

FAILING FORWARD

Craig Groeschel uses a term I like for failure. He calls it "failing forward."[6] We need to learn to fail forward. And grace makes it possible to fail forward. Some failure is a result of sin that has taken hold in our lives. Other kinds of failure have nothing to do with sin. Failure accompanies trying new things, dreaming, taking on new challenges, taking necessary risks, stepping out for God, or just living life. Groeschel reinforces the principle that if you are going to succeed in what God has called you to, part of that journey will be failure and being able to move on from that failure. It is through failure that you learn, grow, break through walls, and shatter paradigms. "Failure is not an option. It is essential … Failure is a part of success."[7] It takes you where you would not otherwise go.

Janna's Story

I'm stuck. I've been stuck for over a year. While it sounds confusing, my life screeched to a halt when I chose to obey God by walking away from the very relationship He had blessed me with. I was hurt, confused, and angry that God had led me so close to marriage just to take it all away from me, especially since I was seeking His will every step of the way. And yet, I knew that this recent relationship had opened up old wounds that had lain dormant for twelve years. Through this relationship, God had brought to light my need to find true healing.

At fourteen years old I was an average grade nine girl, excited for high school and into socializing with friends. I grew up in a Christian home with parents who instilled biblical values in me. I had a confident base in my relationship with Jesus; but the world of high school with all its pressures gradually pulled me from my moorings, and I started slipping away from God. I had an outgoing, fun-loving, go-with-the-flow personality, which led me into a relationship with a boyfriend. At first it was no big deal. We did what normal teens do: movies, walks in the park; it was fun and non-serious. But as our feelings for each other grew, so did the physical expression of those feelings with one another. Our physical intimacy reached a level that I was not prepared for. At the time, for me, it wasn't about how far our intimacy went—it was the realization that it exposed some very deep pain within me. My life crashed down around me as I connected this experience to my grandfather and his uncomfortable embraces; his wandering hands; his deluded expression of affection. I thought I knew what abuse was; surely such minimal contact was not abuse … just the way men get when they grow old. But my head spun out of control and my stomach heaved with sickness. I broke up with my boyfriend almost immediately and plunged into four years of alcohol and drug abuse.

My typical teenage experimenting with alcohol and drugs turned into a full-blown escape from the pain I was feeling. I remember crying out to God and hearing no reply. I recall feeling the pain and hurt but receiving no comfort. I remember all the questions but got no answers. God seemed to be sitting back and watching me self-destruct.

Weekend partying with friends usually consisted of one goal … getting drunk, even plastered. My pain remained undetected by my friends. But they soon grew tired of my uncontrolled drunkenness and knew nothing of the hours that I would drink alone. These binges provided an outlet for my pain and allowed me to block out the powerful feelings of guilt, despair, and hopelessness. But I was spiralling downward. Finally, trips to the hospital shook my parents, who discovered my drinking and tried to stop it. They sought help for me and, although I had left the church, my parents had many people praying for me.

Alcohol brought me temporary relief, but it always wore off and the emptiness would return. I felt so ashamed of my feelings; many people experienced much worse than I had, but here I was—drowning in my hurt. I tried to convince myself that what I had experienced was not real abuse compared to the abuse and horror stories I had seen on *Oprah* or read about in books. I hoped this logic would bring some mental relief. But the battle in my mind continued as this logic could not compete with the intensity of my pain. It still existed. And now my recent breakup confirmed the facts.

4 Looking Back from the Wall

WHEN YOU HIT THE WALL, A PENETRATING QUESTION DRUMS AWAY in the mind. How will I ever be able to move forward again? The reality is that, before you go forward, you will probably have to go back. I just got back from a mayor's prayer breakfast where Dale Lang gave a moving message on forgiveness. Early in the morning on April 28, 1999, Dale and his son Jason went for a drive. Jason had bought an old black Camaro, and he wanted to share the experience with Dad. They had a good time together. A good start to the day. As they parted company, Jason called out, "See you after school, Dad." It was the last time Dale would speak to his son.

Taber, Alberta, was a quiet town. But, that day, it lost its innocence. A fourteen-year-old boy walked into W. R. Meyers High School with a sawed-off .22 calibre rifle. The young man had been the object of teasing and bullying at school, and today was judgment day for him. Jason and two friends just happened to round the corner of a school corridor and walk down the hall toward the young gunman without suspecting what they were approaching. At random, the gunman suddenly raised his rifle and fired four shots in the direction of the three students. Two of the shots missed entirely. One bullet wounded Jason's friend. A fourth shot fatally wounded Jason in the chest.

Later that day, Jason's parents received the news that is every parent's nightmare. They rushed to the hospital where a doctor confronted them with the word that their son had not made it. It was devastating news!

That day, everything changed for the Langs. Dale paced outside the door of the room where his son lay. He was overwhelmed with a sense of loss and grief. He could feel a wall of anger rising up within him. Who had the right to take his son's life … just like that? Who had the right to devastate his family at will? But then he began to ask himself, "What am I going to do with these feelings of anger? How am I going to be able to move forward from here?" He knew from within himself and from his understanding of the Scriptures that forgiveness was the answer. He understood how Jesus had looked out from the cross over those who crucified and mocked Him and expressed those remarkable, incredible words, *"Father, forgive them, for they don't know what they are doing"* (Luke 23:34). Dale didn't feel it. But he knew that forgiveness was a choice. And that day, Dale chose to forgive the young man who had just shot and killed his son.

The memorial service was poignant and agonizing. Dale and his wife were acutely aware of the need of healing in both the school body and the community. As a result, they chose to conduct the service at W. R. Meyers High School. At the close of the service, the Lang family proceeded down the hallway to the very spot where Jason had been gunned down. They prayed and forgave. Dale prayed for the young gunman's family and for the young man himself, that he would be able to make something of his life. It moved a town. It generated a spirit of forgiveness in the town of Taber, unravelling the growing spirit of anger. Forgiveness is powerful and freeing.

A quarter of the book of Genesis is the story of the young man, Joseph. We have already met him. Joseph grew up in a complex, blended, dysfunctional family. A family broken by favouritism, jealousy, and anger, all under one roof. At just seventeen years old, Joseph was betrayed by his brothers, uprooted from his home and all that was familiar, and taken in shackles to Egypt. Joseph's brothers later testified to the terror and anguish in his eyes and the pleading from his lips as they turned their heads and abandoned him. In Egypt, he was enslaved, falsely accused of rape, and wrongly imprisoned. If anyone should have been emotionally and irreparably damaged, it should have been Joseph. So why wasn't he?

LIVING MEMORIES

In his book, *Healing for Damaged Emotions*, David Seamands likens the painful experiences of the past to the growth rings of a tree. One growth ring tells the story of blight and disease. Others chronicle damage due to wind, storm, or fire. Another ring shows a period of drought or even too much rain. Another ring gives account to a year of normal growth. Beneath the bark is the record of everything—the good, bad, and ugly.

But there's a difference between a tree and a person. Now, that was an insightful statement, wasn't it? People are living souls. That means we have a mind, emotions, and a will. That means the events and experiences of life, especially the negative ones, have a profound effect upon us. "In the rings of our thoughts and emotions, the record is there; the memories are recorded, and all are alive. And they directly and deeply affect our concepts, our feelings, our relationships. They affect the way we look at life and God, at others and ourselves."[1] If the rings of your life that record the past are not properly dealt with, you will soon discover that your mind and emotions are trapped there.

LIVING IN THE PAST TENSE

Peter Scazzero, in his book *Emotionally Healthy Spirituality*, reminds us of one of Charles Dickens' characters in the novel *Great Expectations*. Her name was Miss Havisham, the daughter of a wealthy man. She seemed a strange sort of character. She always wore a wedding dress and one shoe. The clocks in her house remained set at a fixed time. Many years earlier, on the day of her wedding, she was busily engaged in getting herself ready for the big event. Her bridal dress was on. She had one shoe on her foot. The clock showed 8:40 AM. That was when the letter arrived. A letter from her husband to be that he was canceling the wedding. She was crushed. Her life was suspended. She stopped all the clocks in the house at 8:40 AM. She spent the rest of her life in her fading wedding dress and one shoe, crippled by that one injurious calamity.[2]

That is how some people live. They live through the present and future in the past tense. The body moves in the present, but the mind is emotionally crushed, crippled, and mired in the mud of the past.

BREAKING THE POWER OF THE PAST: ACCEPTANCE

Usually, to go forward, you need to go back. You need to make peace with your past so it won't mess up your present or future. Two critical steps will break the power of the past. In Genesis 45:5–9, Joseph stated six times that God was behind everything that had happened to him. He recognized that God had sent him and had come to understand the purpose for it all. I would like to further comment on this later in the book, but let it suffice for now to say that Joseph had come to the place of acceptance.

This is the first step one must take to break the power of the past—acceptance of what has occurred. Acceptance means you don't need to fight it any more. Acceptance means you cannot change what has happened and that you choose to believe that God has a dream for your good and for His glory through what has happened.

FORGIVENESS

You won't go back too far before you discover the second step. Forgiveness. You will uncover someone you have to forgive. You may have to forgive God. That doesn't mean God has done something wrong. He hasn't. But I often speak with people who are angry at God for what He has allowed. They say, "God could have stopped it, couldn't He?" "God could have altered the outcome." "He could have kept that from happening. Couldn't He?" Forgiving God is more about us. It is admitting you don't understand, but accepting that God does. It is letting God be God. It is submission to Him.

You may have to forgive yourself. I have already discussed that most difficult process. It's a huge step. But I reemphasize that self-forgiveness is absolutely essential.

You will most definitely find other people you need to forgive. As you read on in Joseph's life, you see his staggering rise to power and authority as governor of Egypt. Read about it in Genesis 40–41. You witness God's providential hand in an amazing way. I'll look more closely at that later as well. But one day, as Joseph was going about his royal imperial duties, preparing to distribute food and provisions to the needy coming to him from all over the known world, something incredible happened.

When the royal doors opened, there before him stood his brothers. As they bowed before him, he recognized them instantly. His betrayers. The very brothers who had so traumatized and injured him. All the pain of the past came rushing back. His heart pounded. His lower lip began to quiver. He could feel the tears welling up inside of him. But he remained stately and imposing. They did not recognize him. I mean, you can imagine this was the last place they would ever expect to find their little brother. And he did not give away his identity. That would come, but not yet. First, he needed to discover their hearts.

It is evident that Joseph now had the authority and power to take revenge and punish all those who had treated him so wrongly. But there is no evidence that he ever did so. Not to Potiphar, his first master, who had unjustly thrown him into prison and thrown away the keys. Not to Potiphar's wife, who had laid those false charges that landed him in the prison for so many years. And now, not to his brothers. Those closest to you can hurt you the most. Forgiveness is usually not felt. Forgiveness is an act of your will. You choose to do so, or not. Joseph chose to forgive. It had been many years, but there is no statute of limitations on forgiveness.

When the suitable time came for Joseph to reveal his identity, it was a heart-stopping, heartrending moment. Joseph's tears flowed like a downpour from a broken cloud. He wept so loudly that his sobs could be heard throughout the palace. His brothers stood there, mouths gaping open. They stared at the man before them, stunned and speechless as this surreal moment unfolded before them. Joseph encouraged them not to feel angry or anguished, for he would care and provide for them and their families. His words were the evidence of complete and total forgiveness.

Several years later, when father Jacob had died, the brothers became fearful again that Joseph would take revenge. With Dad gone, they now felt no buffer between themselves and Joseph. But Joseph was quick to reassure them with heartfelt tears that there was no need to fear him. He spoke kindly to them, *"Don't be afraid of me. Am I God, that I can punish you? You intended to harm me, but God intended it all for good … I will continue to take care of you and your children"* (Genesis 50:19–21). Again, his words and actions were the evidence of genuine forgiveness.

We learn a lot about forgiveness from Joseph. Forgiveness does not deny or condone sinful actions, but it does refuse to play God. It refuses to be judge. It refuses to pay back or to hold against. It chooses, rather, to let go, even going the next step and showing care.

One day, the disciple Peter asked Jesus if there was any limitation on the number of times that one should forgive an offender. Jesus said no. It is easier to hold a grudge, to want to get even. It is so much easier to nurse a hurt, and to feel self-pity. But Jesus replied, *"Seventy times seven"* (Matthew 18:22). The original word used in this passage is *aphiami*, and it means "to release." Keep releasing. Again, it does not mean to deny or condone sinful actions. It does not mean you should remain in the same hurtful situation. You may need to establish healthy boundaries where you are not vulnerable to hurt. You may need intervention.

Forgiveness, in its true sense, means to release the hurt, to release the right to get even, to release or cancel the debt. And when you choose to forgive, you release a heavy emotional load from your mind and heart. In fact, you will never know true healing from past hurt until you release. When you choose to forgive, you are released from the power and control of the offender. You refuse to remain under the weight of his or her emotional hold. You have, in fact, taken your offender off the hook in your life and placed that person on God's hook. You refuse to carry that person any longer.

Sometimes victims carry their offenders around on their backs for their whole lives, and those offenders get heavier and heavier and heavier. Release them. If there is any judgment for their actions, let God do that. Only then are you released from the control of the past and free to enjoy the present with a new resilience. You are free to move forward with your life.

STORY OF AN UNFORGIVING SERVANT

Forgiveness may be one of the most difficult things you ever do. But let's put it into perspective. Immediately following Jesus' response to Peter's struggle to forgive, He told a story. You can read the whole story in Matthew 18:23–35. A servant was dragged in before his king and told to pay his debt. The debt was up into the millions of dollars, and the servant stood before the king trembling uncontrollably. He was expecting a life sentence. But the king recognized the absolute impossibility of the servant ever paying off the debt. He even felt pity for the man. So he released the man and forgave the debt. Wow! And that's exactly what God did for us.

We owed a debt we could not pay; He paid a debt He did not owe. On the cross, Jesus paid our debt of sin that condemned us to an eternity without God and released us from the punishment and the payment. All you must do is receive His gift of forgiveness, His offer of release, by faith in Jesus' death for you. All you owe is eternal gratitude. And a commitment to give the same gift of forgiveness to others who offend you.

Jesus continued with His story. This same forgiven servant went out and found one of his fellow servants who owed him a few thousand dollars. He grabbed him by the throat and demanded instant payment. His friend, servant number two, begged for a little more time, all to no avail. The passage states that servant number one *"wouldn't wait"* (Matthew 18:30). Forgiveness is a matter of choice. It is not that you cannot; it is that you will not. The friend was thrown into jail. When the other servants saw this, they immediately text-messaged the king's court. The king was angry and had servant number one immediately called in. The king came down hard on the unforgiving servant. *"You evil servant! I forgave you that tremendous debt because you pleaded with me. Shouldn't you have mercy on your fellow servant, just as I had mercy on you?"* (Matthew 18:32–33). The king then had him thrown into prison. Jesus added, *"That's what my heavenly Father will do to you if you refuse to forgive"* (verse 35).

The lesson is obvious. Jesus is drawing a contrast. If God has forgiven your tremendous debt against Him, then you should forgive others of their lesser debts against you. Whatever others owe you, it is less than what you owed God. When you do not forgive, it's because you do not understand the degree of your debt or the depth of God's forgiveness. This is Jesus' perspective on forgiveness. And let's not miss the warning Jesus gave in verse 35. If you will not forgive others, God will not forgive you. Jesus reemphasizes this again at the close of His prayer in Matthew

6:14–15. When you refuse to forgive, you break the bridge over which you must cross one day.

A FORGIVING COMMUNITY

Forgiveness is so powerful. I remember when the story hit the newscast. Charles Roberts was a milk truck driver, thirty-two years old. Back in October 2006, he walked into an Amish school in Lancaster County, Pennsylvania. He dismissed the boys and the teacher and barricaded the doors. He then began to execute the remaining ten girls one by one. Before the police were able to break into the school, he had killed five young girls, severely wounded the other five, and killed himself.

The outside world was shocked. The Amish community went into deep grief. But something else stunned the world even more. It is called grace, or a gift. The Amish believe God is in sovereign control and has an ultimate plan in everything that He allows. They believe, therefore, that the best response to offence is forgiveness.

Seventy-five members of the Amish community attended the funeral of Charles Roberts. They prayed for their own hurting families and for the family of the perpetrator. Jack Meyer, a member of the Amish community, made the astonishing statement that he didn't think there was anyone in the community who wanted to do anything but forgive. Forgiveness trumps violence. Forgiveness touches the world around us. When forgiveness is given, you are most like Jesus. When you forgive, you are released from the emotional hold of the past and freed to begin healing and to move forward.

FORGIVE AND FORGET?

It is interesting that Joseph had forgiven his offenders years before his brothers showed up. He had two sons. The eldest son he named Manasseh. Manasseh means, "God made me forget my troubles and family." You've heard the phrase "forgive and forget." The apostle Paul used the word *forget* in Philippians 3:13: *"I focus on this one thing:* forgetting *the past and looking forward to what lies ahead"* (emphasis added).

To forget doesn't mean you experience a loss of the mental and psychological capacity to remember. It doesn't mean you've come down with amnesia. Paul had a lot in his life—before he became a believer in Christ—that he would have given anything to forget. He had harassed, hunted, and hurt those who followed the Way. The sound of children crying as they were torn from their parents' arms during midnight raids. The sound of skulls cracking under the pummeling of stones. Our minds want to play the tapes of failure, hurt, and woundedness over and over again. And they don't seem to wear out; they just seem to wear in. The tapes wear deep grooves into our minds.

I remember—while travelling in the Kingdom of Jordan—walking down a street in the ancient city of Jerash. White marble pillars lined the sides, but carved into the aged stones of the ancient road were the grooves of chariot wheels that had rolled up and down the street two thousand years ago. Those furrows took one back to the ancient past. For an historian, that is an amazing experience. But when it comes to the memories that the mind and emotions need to forget, the grooves are ruts of the past that trap you in their hold and control where you are going.

To forget means the same as *to forgive*: to let go. Again, not in an amnesic sense, but in not allowing any emotional control. Let go of the memories of hurts and losses; they can get so heavy. Of failures; they don't mean that *you* are a failure. Of successes; they are no guarantee of success in the future. Of the bad memories that still threaten to traumatize you. Of the good memories of the "good old days" that chain you to the past with strong feelings over what *was* and prevent you from accepting what *is* with resilience and joy. When your memories exceed the strength and energy of your dreams, you wear an emotional chain to your past.

FORGIVENESS, THE CHOICE THAT LIBERATES

On December 20, 1974, Chris Carrier, a fifth-grade boy, was on his way home from school for the Christmas holidays. He had just been dropped off by the school bus. A man approached him, pretending to be a family friend, and lured him to his motor home. They travelled north out of Miami. Chris had just been abducted. He was stabbed multiple times with an ice pick inside the motor home. Chris was still alive as the man drove until dusk out into the Everglades. He stopped the vehicle and led Chris a little way from the road. He drew a revolver, placed it against the temple of Chris' head, pulled the trigger, and left the boy for dead. The bullet severed the optic nerve of Chris' left eye. For six days Chris lay in a coma. For six days, the police searched and found nothing. For six days Chris lay without shelter from the elements or wild animals.

At dusk on the sixth day, a hunter discovered him. By God's grace, Chris had survived what seemed to be the inconceivable. He was able to give a description of his assailant to a police sketch artist. This led to the quick arrest of David McAllister. The forensics of the day, however, did not give the evidence necessary for a conviction. Young Chris was not able to give a positive ID. McAllister was released on lack of evidence.

Twenty years later, a policeman who had worked the case was visiting a nursing home and recognized McAllister lying in a bed. He was bedridden and blind. The officer told McAllister that he was no longer in danger of punishment and encouraged him to confess to the crime so that the family could have some closure. He did. Chris Carrier was informed and asked if he wanted to see the man. Chris answered in the affirmative. He believed he had already forgiven the man and was prepared to confront him. As he stood before McAllister, he did not identify himself. Initially the man refused to admit any wrongdoing. Upon further questioning, however, the man began to weep and admitted his crime. At that point, Chris identified himself as the boy McAllister had abducted and injured. Over the next six days, Chris visited the man five times.

Chris told McAllister that he forgave him. He shared about his faith and his relationship with Jesus Christ. He befriended him. He asked questions about McAllister's life. He tried to get beneath him. Chris informed him that he had not robbed him of anything. He built a relationship with his offender and in time led him to faith in Christ. Three weeks after this event, David McAllister died.

Many may find it hard to believe that Chris was able to forgive the one who had stabbed and shot him.

> This experience left me with a choice: Do I look at myself as a victim of a tragic set of circumstances that has left me physically scarred and emotionally changed, or do I look at myself as the receiver of blessings beyond belief? I should have been killed by David McAllister when he stabbed me many times with an ice pick. I should have been killed when I was shot in the head at point-blank range. If I was not killed immediately, I should have bled to death in the six days I lay there. It was December. I had no shelter. The elements could have killed me, if not the wild animals in the area. I choose to consider myself the receiver of miracles and blessings. By the grace of God, David McAllister failed, but Christ died on the cross and was victorious for all time. Because of that victory, I can forgive.[3]

I began this chapter by sharing that I had just returned from a prayer breakfast where Dale Lang shared his story about forgiveness. He also said that you know you've forgiven when you can think about the offender and still feel peace in your mind. You think about the offender, and you wish the best for him or her. Forgiveness releases. You release the offender, and you are released from the offender. You've broken his or her power and control over you. You are free to bless. Free to love. Free to enjoy life. Free to move forward.

Rebecca's Story

I HAD ALWAYS WANTED A BIG FAMILY. LOTS OF CHILDREN. INFERTILITY had never entered my mind. Pregnancy is one of the most natural things in a woman's life. But, now, here I was heading off to another doctor … further monitoring … an alternative procedure … different medication … more surgery. And still I could not get pregnant. I felt broken.

I was having a personal struggle with God. After I shed many tears in my husband's arms and after I placed many phone calls with more tears to my parents, they suggested that I start keeping a journal. A written testimony of my feelings, questions, and anger towards God. A record of my journey. They gave me an empty journaling notebook and, after some hesitation, I began to write.

> January 6
>
> Today is the first day I actually decided to write in my journal. We have just started to pursue the adoption route. Chris (my husband), my family, and I fasted in prayer several days ago. I have mixed feelings about everything. But I have decided to leave it all in God's hands and wait to see what happens. God is definitely taking us on a journey. Some of it has been great. For other parts I've been so angry, frustrated, upset, and confused. I feel like my eyes have been blindfolded. I need to keep moving forward, but I don't know where to go.

> January 22
>
> Nobody understands how sad I feel inside. I want a baby so badly. I feel so hopeless. I don't know where to go with this. I don't know what God is trying to tell me. And I am looking so hard for His guidance. I just don't feel that He is there. I don't understand why He is doing this to me. And I know people will tell me that God does love me and that there is a reason for everything. But I can't stand this!!!!! I just wish that God would somehow show me that He is there and that He does hear … because right now I don't feel it. NOT AT ALL. I FEEL SO ALONE!!

Listening to worship songs gave me a peace and comfort. I truly felt God speaking to me through them. My mother gave me an article written by Matt and Beth Redman. The Redmans are songwriters and worship leaders and had written a book, *Blessed Be Your Name,* inspired in part by a series of painful miscarriages. I felt particularly encouraged by their words. They wrote,

> Life on earth can be a tough and painful journey. Yet it's a journey in which God calls us to worship Him in every circumstance and assures us that His grace will be sufficient. Our heavenly Father doesn't promise escape from pain in this world, yet He proves Himself ever faithful to those who choose to trust Him. Every act of worship is a decision to believe and respond to God for who He says He is—no matter how pressing our circumstances. And the greater the pain we're experiencing, the tougher the choice may be.

I realized that to trust God and worship Him was not always a feeling; it was a choice that I had to make. I made that choice.

After three years of being infertile, we were blessed with a beautiful son. But I know it doesn't always work out that way. My heart feels the pain that many women experience at the wall of infertility. I have a poem on my fridge to help me through those tough days. I share it with you who are suffering today.

As children bring their broken toys,
With tears for us to mend,
I brought my broken dreams to God,
Because He is my friend.
But then instead of leaving Him
In peace to work alone,
I hung around and tried to help,
With ways that were my own.
At last, I snatched them back again
And cried, "How can you be so slow?"
"My child," He said, "What could I do?"

—Source Unknown

5 Looking Up from the Wall

We come to a very important chapter. Recently, I received a phone call from a close friend. He had gone to see his doctor to check into a problem he had been told was probably minor in nature. But it wasn't minor. It was cancer. He had hit the wall. Six weeks later, my friend was dead.

There are times when we hit a wall and have nowhere to look but up. It could be cancer, infertility, divorce, loss of a job, loss of a loved one, or one of many other losses. We feel so totally at the end of ourselves with no answers that we just look up with longing eyes. The psalmist wrote, *"I look up to the mountains—does my help come from there? My help comes from the Lord who made heaven and earth!"* (Psalm 121:1–2). Note how the psalmist draws on a divine perspective. When I look up, I recognize that my help comes from the Lord. He is no pagan mountain god. He is the One who created the mountains, yea, the whole earth and the vast heavens. And if He can do all of that, then He can help me with my struggle and need. Relative to anything, God is bigger.

BEHIND THE CURTAIN

Let's think back to Joseph again. Joseph had plenty of reason to say, "My life is a mistake." "I can never trust anyone ever again." "I don't want to feel; it's too painful." But he didn't. He could have set his sights on himself and felt a debilitating self-pity. He didn't. He could have set his sights on people who had hurt or rejected him and felt a deepening emotional distancing or a desire for revenge. He didn't. Joseph had hit a thirteen-year-thick wall of betrayal and injustice. But he refused to do what so many people do, to simply act out the script handed to them by the past, by life, by others. To simply acquiesce to "what is, is." Instead, he looked up!

There is no way Joseph could have understood everything that was happening in his life. But he knew that God was behind the curtain somewhere. As noted earlier, he understood that God had sent him to Egypt for a purpose. The verse that sums up Joseph's life is Genesis 50:20: *"You intended to harm me,* but *God intended it all for good. He brought me to this position so I could save the lives of many people"* (emphasis added). We know the full story and outcome of Joseph's life from Scripture. Joseph didn't have that advantage. But he believed God was bringing good out of evil and chose to embrace the new meaning God was bringing into his life.

For thirteen years, Joseph encountered a "dark night of the soul."[1] As noted earlier in chapter 2, this term was coined by St. John of the Cross many years ago in 1585. John wrote about how you can know when you are encountering a "dark night of the soul." Peter Scazzero summarizes John's reflections by breaking them down into six distinctives. The sense of God's presence evaporates. One's prayers seem to go unanswered; heaven seems silent. One feels darkness, defeat, emptiness; there is a longing to quit. The spiritual disciplines you relied on before no longer work for you; you're not getting anything out of reading your Bible—in fact, you aren't reading it. You cannot fathom or make sense of what God might be doing. Finally, you see little visible fruit in your life.[2]

Have you been there? Maybe that's where you are right now. While the light dawned for Joseph after his thirteen years of darkness, I'm sure that many times during those years he felt the presence of these realities dragging him down. He felt the sting of his brothers' harm, *"but God..."* I like that. He disciplined himself to look up even when there seemed little reason to. And he became an inspiring example for us all.

A MYSTERIOUS GOD

You hit the wall. You lie on your back, stunned, broken. You open your eyes. And you are looking up. After you've calculated the damage, the first thought that will probably become embedded in your mind is a question. Why?

Good question. But not so easy to answer, because you quickly discover something about God. You discover that God is clouded in mystery. God is mysterious. You can attain a degree of understanding about God from Scripture, nature, and life. But He is far more. You are only scratching the surface.

In Isaiah 40:13–14, the prophet asks, *"Who is able to advise the Spirit of the Lord? Who knows enough to give Him advice or teach Him? … Does He need instruction about what is good?"* The answer, of course, is an unequivocal *no!* Further down the chapter, Isaiah reminds us that *"God sits above the circle of the earth. The people below seem like grasshoppers to him"* (verse 22). God, the Holy One, asks, *"To whom will you compare me? Who is my equal?"* (verse 25). God's infinite mind, knowledge, wisdom, and ways are incalculably beyond what our small finite minds can grasp. *"'My thoughts are nothing like your thoughts,' says the Lord. 'And my ways are far beyond anything you could imagine. For just as the heavens are higher than the earth, so my ways are higher than your ways and my thoughts higher than your thoughts'"* (Isaiah 55:8–9).

God is infinite *light.* But we read that Moses entered the thick *darkness* where God was (Exodus 20:21). Try to work that out in your head. God is *transcendent,* meaning that He is so far above us that human thought cannot imagine. But He is *imminent,* so close that He is always present. God is *eternal*—He has no created beginning and existence; He is timeless, living in the eternal *now.* We do not have the capacity to fully understand God.

Scazzero stated it well:

> I like control. I like to know where God is going, exactly what he is doing, the exact route of how we are getting there, and exactly when we will arrive. I also like to remind God of his need to behave in ways that fit in with my clear ideas of

> him. For example, God is just, merciful, good, wise, loving. The problem, then, is that God is beyond the grasp of every concept I have of him. He is utterly incomprehensible.[3]

We can ask why, we can try to make sense, we can try to discover the good, but we often have no idea what God is doing.

GOODNESS NEVER ENDS

Several years ago, our daughter Rebecca and her husband hit a wall. Infertility. You read her story at the beginning of this chapter. They suffered the loss of a preterm baby, adoption loss, and the loss of the ability to get pregnant. This is a wall that many couples hit, and the sense of loss is deep. For many of these couples, it is a lonely experience. People will pray for you if you are ill, or in hospital, or if you are going through a divorce or have lost your job. But not necessarily if you are suffering from infertility. In fact, the responses from well-meaning people are commonly, "Well, you've got one child." Or, "God knows best." It's one of those things that others have a difficult time understanding in terms of loss—until they themselves (or someone close to them) experience it.

For Rebecca and Chris, it meant an endless round of visits to doctors, fertility treatments, lots of encouragement and prayer. In the end we celebrated the birth of a beautiful miracle-baby boy. This little guy was and still is one of our most profound delights. But it doesn't always turn out this way.

Another young woman, a friend of our family, got pregnant at the same time as our daughter. Same due dates. This second young woman had already lost six babies due to miscarriages. Now, she was pregnant with number seven. We also prayed for her alongside praying for our daughter. We prayed and prayed and prayed. We were encouraged as she carried her baby one month, two months, right up to nine months. One week to go! And then her baby's heart stopped. It just stopped! We were stunned. We got the phone call at the same time we were preparing to run to the hospital to welcome our new little grandson. Romans 12:15 instructs us to *"be happy with those who are happy and weep with those who weep.*" But all in one day? Sometimes. In one week we celebrated the birth of one little boy and mourned the loss of a little girl.

We sent a card to our grieving friends. A card that we choose at times like this. A special card. It is a copy of an acrylic painting that was done by another dear friend of ours, Karyn Percival. Earlier, you read Ian's story. Karyn was Ian's mother. Karyn was a talented artist. She had a passion for life, learning, and Christ. She called herself a "Visual Missionary," using diverse imagery to share the joy of her own spiritual journey. She used her art as a means of moving people's hearts with a spiritual message. One spring day, Karyn tragically fell from a cliff while hiking in Algonquin Park, not far from our home. Her death was grievous, but her paintings are part of the rich legacy she left for us.

The painting on the card to which I referred was titled "Goodness Never Ends." The dominant colour is red. But there are many other colours blended in. Blues. Yellows. Greens. Orange. Black. In fact, black is a prevailing colour, attaching itself to all the other colours. Now, Karyn would have been the first person to tell you that the meaning of the picture is open to interpretation. So, while you might interpret it differently, I have come up with my own interpretation. Hence, I used this card to communicate with our grieving friends.

> So much in life is a mystery. So much about God is a mystery. His ways transcend our minds' capacity. The painting on this card is a picture of our lives. The splashes of bright and diverse colours depict the many joys and happy times that make up our lives. These are the obvious reminders of God's goodness and faithfulness. Life is not all sorrowful. But then there are the prevailing black brush marks affixed to all the other colours. Embedded into the mix of our lives is the sorrowful, the tearful, the tragic, the unavoidable. However, the dominant colour is red, the colour of blood. A reminder of Jesus' pain at Calvary and of how much He loves you. A reminder that He understands your pain and loss. Our pain, loss, and grief are on the same canvas as God's love, faithfulness, and goodness, even though the "why" usually remains a mystery.

A fruit of hitting the wall is the cultivation of a childlike acceptance of mystery. I can't understand. But He understands. Therefore I will look up and rest in Him.

A PREVAILING PRESENCE

God is clouded in mystery, but He is present, always present. That's another great truth you will discover about God when you look up. God's presence was something Joseph understood. In Genesis 39, you read four times that during those years of adversity *"the LORD was with Joseph."* That reassurance is given multiple times in Scripture. In Hebrews 13:5, God says, *"I will never fail you. I will never abandon you."* It doesn't show up in the English, but in the Greek the reassurance shows up as a triple negative. In other words, "I will never, never, never abandon you." "I will not, I will not, I will not ever abandon you." It's as if the Holy Spirit is saying, "Get the point? Don't ever doubt this!"

It makes a difference when you know who is with you. Bill Hybels parallels God's prevailing presence to the presence of a parent for a child in the middle of the night.[4] Every parent has experienced the sound of that still, small voice in the night. You are deep in sleep. You feel a little hand rest on your shoulder. Your head is more than foggy. You peer at the digital clock. It is 2:33 AM.

"Daddy, I have to go to the bathroom."

"Thanks for the update, son," you reply. "It's just down the hall where it was last night."

Now, to a four-year-old, the hall is a mile long. There are multiple doors leading out into the hall, from which any one of them can loom a three-headed monster or a wild animal on the prowl for little boys on their way to the bathroom.

You hear him shuffle away. But then you hear those shuffles return to your bedside.

"Will you come with me?" returns the little voice.

"Thanks for the invitation, son, but can you do it on your own?"

You know the answer. So you pull your feet from under the covers, get out of bed, and take him by the hand. It makes all the difference to your child to know that Dad is with him. Dad's presence dispels the fear.

You are the child in that long, dark hallway. You are anxious about the risks, apprehensive about the distance, afraid of the potential obstacles, and feel fearful. But your Father is with you. If you believe that, it makes all the difference.

A REFUGE

No one understood this more than David, the psalmist. When he wrote Psalm 62, he was being harassed by his enemies. They looked at him as a *"broken-down wall,"* and they wanted to topple him. They praised him to his face, but then told lies behind his back (verses 3–4). This may have been the time in David's life when he was hiding from the relentless pursuit of King Saul. For thirteen years, he hid out in the Judean wilderness, a harsh, inhospitable tangle of ravines and caves, a place that could be deathly silent as all life hid from the relentless heat of the sun. But he had come to Engedi, an oasis on the edge of the wilderness down near the Dead Sea. At Engedi were water and a cave—cool, refreshing, safe. David found God there. *"I wait quietly before God … He alone is my rock and my salvation, my fortress where I will never be shaken"* (verses 1–2). He repeats those word pictures again in verses 5 and 6. Rock. Fortress. He uses another word picture in verses 7 and 8. Refuge.

You need to understand the difference between the Eastern mind and the Western mind. The Eastern mind spoke in pictures. Concepts were rich in imagery. Whereas we would say with our Western mindset that God is powerful, the Eastern mind would picture God as "my Rock." Whereas we would say the Lord leads and guides us, the Eastern mind would use the imagery of a shepherd leading me to green pastures, still streams, or through the valley of darkness. The Lord is my Shepherd. We would speak of Christ as our source of life; they would say that Christ is the vine and we are the branches, because branches receive their life from the vine. The psalmist habitually used the imagery of a refuge to express the presence of God. A refuge was a cave or any place to which he could run and hide from the pressing demands, challenges, adversities, and perils of life. *"[God] is my refuge, a rock where no enemy can reach me … Trust in him at all times. Pour out your heart to him, for God is our refuge"* (Psalm 62:7–8).

A refuge is a place to embrace when you hit the wall. More so, it is the painful experiences in life that lead you there. When you are running for your life, you need to be running to God, your refuge. Eugene Peterson reflects on the word *refuge.* "*Refuge* refers to a good experience, but what got [David] to refuge was a bad experience. He started out running for his life; and at some point he found the life he was running for, and the name for that life was God."[5]

The psalmist paints a beautiful picture of God as our refuge in Psalm 91:4: *"He will cover you with his feathers. He will shelter you with his wings."* Some years ago, when my children were young, we visited a local zoo. There was a duck sitting close to the fence, and my son, like most little boys would, gently poked her with a small twig. The duck jumped up and out from under her scampered a dozen little ducklings. They had been covered under the shelter of her wings, in the dark, trusting, resting. What a beautiful word picture for any who are oppressed, wounded, weak, afraid, lonely, discouraged, or grieving. He shelters you under His wings. You trust. You rest in safety and security. And He promises that He will never abandon you.

Only one person was ever abandoned by God. Jesus watched in silence as His friends forsook Him. When His enemies tortured Him, He forgave them. But when His Father in heaven turned His back, it broke Jesus' heart. He opened His parched lips and uttered the lament, *"My God, my God, why have you abandoned me?"* (Matthew 27:46). God had to turn His back on Christ because He was carrying all of our sin—every deplorable, despicable, vile, shameful sin that had ever been committed or ever would be. He carried it all, alone—absolutely alone! But because He was willing to carry and pay for our sin, we can be reconciled to God. Because He was abandoned by God, no believer will ever be abandoned by God.

We have a wonderful promise from the resurrected, ascended Jesus, who is in heaven today and is intently interested in what is happening in your life.

> *This High Priest of ours understands our weaknesses, for he faced all of the same testings we do, yet he did not sin. So let us come*

> *boldly to the throne of our gracious God. There we will receive his mercy, and we will find grace to help us when we need it the most* (Hebrews 4:15–16).

I think of all the people who look up from the wall with despairing eyes. I picture tears glazing Jesus' eyes, as a scarred hand lifts to wipe away a tear rolling down His cheek. And while the *why* may remain a mystery, He whispers, "I feel your pain. I understand. I won't abandon you, and My grace will get you through this."

A DIVINE HAND

One of the most amazing things for me when I look up from the wall is how involved the God of the universe is in the details of my life. I can't imagine all the vigilance it takes to keep this universe operating. Or all of the attention He must have to give to this world just to keep it from imploding. Yet, He is so profoundly involved and interested in me and you. There are the times of obvious divine involvement and intervention. The times when you can unmistakably see and feel the hand of God. And then there are the myriad occasions and junctures in your life that have no visible linkage to the hand of God but which, all multiplied together, disclose a hidden divine hand at work behind the scenes. These are the things we call coincidence. It's amazing, when God is doing something in your life, how much coincidence there is.

There's a word attributed to God that embraces His involvement in our lives. The word is *providential. Providence* comes from the Latin. To understand its meaning, just break the word into two parts. *Pro* means "before." *Video* is the verb "to see." So *providence* means to "see before." If you look for the root word embedded in providence, you find the word *provide.* Putting it all together, *providence* means that God sees ahead in your life. He sees what is around the next corner, and the next, and He provides. There is a hidden, divine hand that guides all things from beginning to end, superintending, causing, affecting, and managing your life—and providing. Wow!

Joseph certainly understood the providential involvement of God in his life. All through those years of adversity, the Scriptures inform us that God *was present with* Joseph, *made* Joseph successful, *sent* Joseph into Egypt to preserve lives, *made* him a counsellor to Pharaoh, *intended* everything that happened to Joseph to turn to good, and *brought* him to this position of ruler to save lives. God was writing the script for Joseph's life and bringing new meaning to his existence.

DIVINE INTERVENTION

During the time when I hit my first overwhelming wall, I felt like I was in an emotional life-and-death struggle. If it had not been for the providential involvement of God in my life, I would not have survived. I left the ministry, disillusioned with church, people, and, most of all, myself. I sent out dozens of résumés, all to no avail. God seemed to be blocking everything. Was God punishing me? I began wondering if God had abandoned me. I had my wife and three young children to provide and care for. What would I do? There is no deeper despair than the thought that God may have abandoned you. Of course, He hadn't. But heaven seemed silent.

That year, we moved a total of six times. Six homes. I felt like Abraham, moving his tent from place to place to place in a land that was not his own. We lived on handouts and the generosity of other people. When there was a need, somehow there was a supply. We seemed to be living the life of the widow who provided for the prophet Elijah. There was always enough flour and olive oil left at the bottom of the barrel. We obviously didn't live in any house for too long. We moved our stuff into one particular place for only ten days. While there was a strong temptation to focus on what we didn't have, it began to dawn on me that God was involved in our lives and providing all along. We hadn't spent one night on the curb. We seemed always to have a roof over our heads and a bed to sleep in. He had not abandoned us. He was very present and active.

One Saturday afternoon, I received a very disheartening phone call. As I put the phone down, I sat for about fifteen minutes, heavyhearted and downcast, but also fighting the debilitating feelings of anger and rejection. Suddenly, the phone rang again. I picked it up hesitantly, not knowing who would be on the other end. It was Bill, a good friend of mine from the past. He had no idea what I had just experienced. He said, "God just told me to call you. He said that you need some encouragement." Talk about God's providential involvement. I looked up.

Another day, there was a rap on the door. A man stood on the steps, and, as I opened the door, he pushed his way in. I tried to stay calm but take charge, not knowing why he had come. He was angry as he sat down and pointed his accusing finger at me. I had no opportunity to speak as he made false accusation after false accusation. I had never experienced anything like this before, and the whole situation seemed surreal. My two young daughters who were not yet school age began to cry hysterically while Diane, my wife, scurried them away. I tried to get control of the situation. I quickly discerned that the words this man spoke were from the devil, the enemy himself, and I ordered him out of our home. He refused. I prayed audibly, pointed to the door, and ordered him out a second time. He got up and left. I was visibly shaken. We all were.

Not five minutes later, after only a brief moment to process what had just happened, the doorbell rang again. My heart jumped. We went to the side window and peered out to see whether the same aggressor had returned. He hadn't. But what we did see astonished us. Another surreal moment. There were two big, broad-shouldered men, dressed head to foot in white. White suits. White boots. And large, white, wide-brimmed Stetsons. We didn't know what to think. These men were either Texas Rangers with a warrant for my arrest or an angelic visitation. I guardedly opened the door, more out of curiosity than anything else.

They greeted me with wide smiles and said in loud, cordial voices, "Are you David?" I nodded. "We've been sent to pray for you." There was no explanation of who they were or where they were from. They invited themselves in (which seemed to be becoming commonplace) and literally, picking me up by the arms, carried me to the living room (it was as if they knew where they were going).

They then plunked me onto my knees, placed their big burly hands on my shoulders, and began praying. And praying. And praying. And praying. They prayed that I would know God's presence in a most real way. That God would fill me with His Spirit, His comfort, hope, joy, assurance, vision, love, strength, and courage. That I would know God's restorative hand in my life. They spoke into my heart as they prayed, telling me to know with certainty that God had a purpose for me, a dream no man could thwart. They prayed divine spiritual protection around me and my family. They prayed on and on. I felt like I was being drawn up into the very presence of God, into heaven itself. When they finished, they got up, lifted me from my knees, and enveloped me in a huge bear hug. I could feel the love and strength of God flowing through them. It was like being hugged by Jesus Himself. The timing was incredible in light of what had occurred just moments earlier. Coincidence? No. I looked up and thanked God for His providential involvement.

THE FLEECE

Several months passed. One evening, two men came to visit Diane and me. They were from a small church about forty kilometres away in a town called Aurora. They had come to ask me if I would consider coming to be their pastor. The thought scared me. I was not looking for any church ministry, especially as a pastor. But as time passed, it became apparent that God had sent them. God was opening a door that no man could shut. To make a long story short, it was the beginning of a relationship with this small church that was to change my life.

I struggled. There were growing uncertainties. Looming deadlines. We had to make a decision. Would I agree to become the pastor of this church and move my family to another location? I believed that God had opened a door, but just the thought of it revived old fears. Reawakened insecurities. Stirred up doubts and apprehension. So I looked up. We prayed, "Lord, clearly show us what to do. If You are really in this, we are willing. But we need to know."

I then did something I had never done before and haven't since. I put out a fleece. I had always thought a fleece showed a lack of faith, but Gideon had done it and God had spoken to him. Not sure whether it was faithful or faithless to do so, but needing an answer from God, we set out our fleece. It had to be something only God could do.

It was April 17. The temperature was supposed to go up to 70 degrees Fahrenheit the next day. We decided on our fleece. If God was calling us to

Aurora, then there should be a layer of white on the ground by morning. We prayed and committed this to God. Seconds later, we could hear the sound of something beating the chimney (I was sitting by the fireplace) and pelting against the windows. I thought it was a wind that had suddenly come up and was striking a heavy rain against the house. We jumped up and ran to look outside. We could hardly believe what our eyes were seeing. It was hailing so heavily that we could not see past the window panes. What's a word for what we felt? Shocked. Amazed. Overwhelmed. I grabbed the camera and rushed outside. The ground was covered with white. I snapped a picture from the door. I guess I was like Gideon at that moment. I prayed, "Lord, if this really is You, then may the white remain until morning in the place where I have just snapped this picture."

It did. I took another picture with the camera the next morning. God had spoken. We have both pictures framed and hanging on the wall. I can see them from here. The kind of pictures that hang on a wall, people stare at with a puzzled look, and finally garner the nerve to ask, "What's that?" Well, that's a reminder that when you hit the wall in your life, you need to look up. Because He is there and is actively and providentially involved in everything that is happening with you.

A SOVEREIGN GOD

Earlier in the book, I talked about Paul's voyage to Rome. It wasn't the most wonderful voyage. It was certainly no Mediterranean cruise. In fact, the whole voyage was a catastrophe. He was sailing on a merchant ship. These ancient merchant ships were a half-walnut shape. The Greeks called this kind of ship a *gaulos*, which means "bathtub." So Paul set off in a supersized bathtub. That's when they hit the mother of all storms. Fourteen days and nights at the mercy of a ferocious nor'easter of typhoon strength. The experienced sailors and crew lost all hope and just let the ship run before the gale.

When I read the story in Acts 28, I again acknowledge God's mysterious nature. God had earlier assured Paul that He would take him to Rome to testify of Him there. But why this way? In chains. In a violent storm. All to end in a shipwreck. Why does God go to all that bother? We can assume an answer. We can say God was doing this or that. But we're not told. It is a mystery. I just know that it's better to be in the storm and in His hands than safe on shore outside His hands.

Then, late one night, an angel of God stood beside Paul. The peace of God's presence appeared in the midst of the storm. The Lord was with him. Not only was the Lord with Paul, but the angel reassured Paul that he would surely stand trial before Caesar in Rome. The storm was not an obstacle to God. You see, behind the storm was a mysterious, unseen, providential, sovereign hand fulfilling His purposes for Paul's life and the kingdom of God.

The backdrop to God's providence is His sovereignty. He is King. He is in absolute control of everything, from the ruling of creation to His rule in your life. A. W. Tozer writes that for God to be sovereign, He must be all-knowing, all-powerful, and absolutely free.

> Were there even one datum of knowledge, however small, unknown to God, His rule would break down at that point … that one stray atom of power would belong to someone else and God would be a limited ruler and hence not sovereign. Furthermore, His sovereignty requires that He be absolutely free … to do whatever He wills to do anywhere at any time to carry out His eternal purpose in every single detail without interference.[6]

When you blend God's absolute sovereignty over your life with His absolute unconditional love for you, the result is security. Whatever wall you hit, whatever storm abruptly blows you out to sea, however unstable or uncertain your life seems, you are secure. Just look up!

Norm's Story

My wife and I hit our wall one night at 10:00 pm. The telephone rang. I knew the voice immediately. It was the dean of men from the university where my son Charles attended. Charles had been in some problematic situations at school that had required some disciplinary action. But when you get a call at 10:00 pm, all sorts of things go through your mind. Has there been some criminal activity? Has my son gone missing? I was wrong.

The gentleman on the other end of the line spoke in a very somber tone and told us that our son had been killed in a motorcycle road accident at six o'clock earlier that evening. He bled to death. He didn't suffer. He knew the Lord as his Saviour. He was in heaven.

I was stunned. All I could say was, "Thank you for calling." I hung up the phone. Our world changed. Our lives would be different from this time on. We hit our wall. Over the next week, it was visiting cemeteries, looking at scores of caskets, arranging a funeral and memorial service, choosing a headstone, answering the phone, receiving friends at our revolving door. Lots of tears. And then long periods of silence as we contemplated, reminisced, grieved, and inwardly bled.

According to the experts, our wall was a big one. Losing a child ranks up there with one of the worst ordeals that one can face. The divorce rate is about 80 percent for couples who have tragically lost a child. I'm glad we survived. We are still married.

We still have our health. We went through a period of real decline about a year later. And we still have times when a deep sense of grief sets in like a fog that obscures the light.

The pain continues to be indescribable. I think of Charles every day. I think about heaven more. I am more aware of my own mortality. I am surviving. I am discovering that my God is bigger than anything.

Perspective at the Wall 6

I could have called this chapter "The Tale of Two Towns." You may be living in one of those towns. And while you may not realize it, the town you're living in is dictating the quality of your life. Two towns. But the same wall. Same challenge. Same opportunity. Same God. And two very different and contrasting outcomes.

KADESH BARNEA: THE PLACE OF HUMAN PERSPECTIVE

The first town is called Kadesh Barnea. The Israelites arrived in this town after making their way from Egypt through the Sinai wilderness. This was their destination. Well, almost. There was one more step. Their real destination was Canaan, the Promised Land, the land God had given to them. Canaan was just over the hill. But it had to be conquered.

Moses sent twelve scouts ahead to explore the land and bring back a report. They returned forty days later with the report that the land was even better than they had ever expected. They showed the people the huge clusters of grapes that hung from the poles shouldered between them. They laid out on the ground pomegranates and figs, samples of the rich produce of the land. The people gasped. Two of the scouts advocated an immediate attack, fully assured of success.

But others disagreed. The other ten spies reported that the towns beyond the hills were large and fortified. There were seven nations living in Canaan, all of them more powerful than Israel. *"We can't go up against them! They are stronger than we are! … The land we traveled through and explored will devour anyone who goes to live there. All the people we saw were huge. We even saw giants there … Next to them we felt like grasshoppers!"* (Numbers 13:31–33). In Deuteronomy 1:28, they reported that the walls of the towns rose high into the sky. Before the Israelites was a herculean wall too formidable to breach. The people were demoralized by this negative report.

The two faithful scouts countered that the Lord their God was going ahead of them and would care for them and fight for them just as they had already seen Him do in Egypt. But the disparaging report had taken root. The people were paralyzed by fear, defeated by unbelief. The motion was moved and passed that they would not budge! God lost the vote. He responded that they *would* budge. Backwards. They would withdraw from the eve of conquest back into the desolate wilderness. The desert would be their home for the next forty years until that first generation had completely died off. The wilderness became a howling graveyard eating up its prey.

THE GRASSHOPPER COMPLEX

The contention was one of perspective. The question weighed was, "How big is your God?" By their very nature, walls stand in front of you like a bully, threatening to crush you if you challenge him. They intimidate you with their presence, size, and strength. They want you to feel like a grasshopper. But they always confront your faith with the question, "How big is your God?" For Israel, the answer was, "Not big enough!" They responded that next to these giants, they felt like grasshoppers (Numbers 13:33). It should have been that "next to our God, these giants are like grasshoppers." But, no. They adopted the grasshopper complex.

This should have been another David and Goliath story. Another Gideon and the Midianites story. I can understand how seven powerful nations armed to the teeth and standing behind walled and fortified cities would be daunting. But this should have been the story of Israel and the Seven Dwarfs—Doc, Grumpy, Bashful, Sleepy, Happy, Sneezy, and Dopey. Remember them? Unfortunately, that was not to be. Israel felt like the grasshopper and turned back.

HOW BIG IS YOUR GOD?

The word *perspective* comes from the Latin word *perspicere,* meaning "to look through." Like looking through a telescope. It means to look through a particular lens and view something relative to something else. To view the size, strength, or beauty of something relative to something else.

A pilot in the cockpit of a huge jumbo jet feels the gigantic size of the jet surrounding him. Comparably, the tarmac below looks no bigger than a piece of pencil lead. His job is to steer this titanic flying ship onto that piece of pencil lead. On the other hand, things look very different on the ground. The air traffic controller on the ground sees the tarmac stretched out before him like a ten-lane interstate highway. The plane looks to him like a speck in the sky. There should be no challenge getting something so small onto something comparably so big. It's a matter of perspective. And sometimes, to acquire a more accurate and reliable picture, we need to look at something from another perspective.

In Isaiah 40:18, the question is asked, *"To whom can you compare God?"* Israel had hit the wall of exile. We could ask, "How big is your God compared to the wall you're facing in your life today?" It is a question of perspective. I have scanned the horizon of the ocean, gazed out over the blowing sands of an endless desert, and stared at the grandeur of a mountain range from an airplane and exclaimed, "Expansive!" But then I compare that to the galaxy in which our planet is located.

Grant Jeffrey gives us an exercise that helps us to obtain a sense of true vastness. Take a piece of paper and draw a dot at the top of the page. The dot represents our earth. Using a scale of one inch to represent ten million miles, draw a small circle nine inches away. This small circle represents our sun. Now, to draw our next neighbouring star, Alpha Centauri, we would have to draw a small circle forty miles away.[1] How long would it take us to travel to Alpha Centauri? Well, let's travel at the speed of light, which is 186,000 miles per second. To give an idea of how fast that is, in the time it takes you to blink an eye, you would have travelled seven and a half times around the world. Now that's lightning fast. Travelling that fast, it would take you about eight and a half minutes to get to our sun. It would take you four and a half years to arrive at Alpha Centauri. It would take you 100,000 years to journey to the other side of our Milky Way galaxy. And the Milky Way is only one galaxy out of an estimated fifty billion galaxies. Now, my perspective on *expansive* has altered. *Expansive* is a matter of perspective.

Stand looking at the curvature of the earth or just do some travelling and you recognize that the earth is big. But then when you compare the size of our earth to another star, Betelguese (pronounced Beetle Juice), a supergiant in the constellation Orion, your perspective on bigness changes. Betelguese alone is twice the size of the earth's orbit around the sun. Now that's big! Bigness is a matter of perspective.

Isaiah asked,

> *To whom can you compare God? … God sits above the circle of the earth. The people below seem LIKE GRASSHOPPERS TO HIM! He spreads out the heavens like a curtain … Look up into the heavens. Who created all the stars? … Because of his great power and incomparable strength, not a single one is missing* (Isaiah 40:18–26, emphasis added).

Isaiah is giving a fresh perspective of the greatness of God. Then he adds the contrast. *"How can you say the LORD does not see your troubles? … But those who trust in the LORD will find new strength. They will soar high on wings like eagles"* (40:27–31). To soar high on wings like an eagle is of significance when you are up against a formidable wall.

Think as big as you can. God is bigger! Sometimes we forget that. We lose perspective.

> *Why are you afraid of mere humans, who wither like the grass and disappear? Yet you have forgotten the LORD, your Creator, the one who stretched out the sky like a canopy and laid the foundations of the earth. Will you remain in constant dread of human oppressors? Will you continue to fear the anger of your enemies?* (Isaiah 51:12–13).

What is bigger, the threat of man who withers like a blade of grass or the hand of God who created all things? What is bigger, the wall that threatens to crush you or the Lord your God? It depends on your perspective. It depends on the lens you're looking through. The natural eye or the lens of faith?

ABEL SHITTIM: THE PLACE OF DIVINE PERSPECTIVE

Kadesh Barnea is not a place where you want to stay. Forty years later, Israel arrived at another town, Abel Shittim. Abel Shittim was situated on the Plains of Moab just east of the Jordan River across from Jericho. The command and challenge was the same. Move into Canaan and conquer it. But this was a new day. A new beginning. A new generation. A new perspective.

The story is recorded in Joshua 3. The land of Canaan lay before the Israelites. But there was another wall. Walls are a reality in life. The Jordan River lay between the nation of Israel and their land of promise. At that particular time of the year, the river overflowed its banks as the steady current emptied its waters into the Dead Sea. How would Joshua, their new leader, get two and a half million people across this obstacle?

The priests followed God's instructions and carried the Ark of God, a sacred box representing the presence of God, with them down the bank and into the water. This was no walk on the beach. This was a faith step. God had instructed them to step down into the river. Only when their feet touched the water at the river's edge would He cut the flow of water off upstream. They stepped over the bank, trying to steady the Ark with their one hand and shoulder as they used the other hand to grasp whatever they could to support themselves. Their feet slid beneath them in the slippery muck as they committed themselves to the Jordan's current. Faith is obeying God by first doing what you can do and then trusting God to do what only He can do.

Walls challenge your faith. They sharpen your perspective that, relative to God, everything is smaller. It was after God had rescued David from all his enemies, including the Philistine giants David had spent years trying to defeat and who had brought him to exhaustion at times, that David wrote a song of praise. In that song he wrote, *"In your strength*

I can crush an army; with my God I can scale any wall" (2 Samuel 22:30). That's a statement of proven faith. The Lord your God is bigger than any wall. Relative to God, everything is smaller. Relative to anything, God is bigger.

I stated earlier that walls are commonplace in our lives. Joshua stepped ashore on Canaan's ground and now faced another wall. A different kind of wall. Walls materialize in all types and stripes. Jericho. A wall of stone, mortar, and military might. Was God bigger than this wall?

Joshua strolled out of camp as the sun fell behind the high rocky cliffs to the west. Jericho stood silhouetted against the deepening red sky. Much rested heavy on his mind. Even after God has met our needs, even miraculously, we still have the challenge of trusting Him for the next time. Joshua stood for a moment, deep in thought, contemplating the next step. Suddenly he heard a noise, and there in front of him was an armed warrior. The sudden sight of the man jolted him out of his thoughts. Joshua quickly drew his sword and commanded the man to identify himself.

He did. *"I am the commander of the LORD's army"* (Joshua 5:14). Joshua slid off his sandals. The place where he stood was holy ground. This was a sacred moment. He was in the presence of the Lord God. The message was clear. Joshua had his eyes and mind set on Jericho's walls. He was to set his heart on God. Joshua was the commander of Israel's army. This one was the commander of the Lord's army. The wall before Joshua was God's challenge, God's problem, God's opportunity. This was all about God. This assurance to Joshua is your assurance today.

You know the story. Israel was ordered to march around Jericho, not against it. This took more faith than courage. On the seventh day, and the thirteenth time marching around the city, *"suddenly, the walls of Jericho collapsed, and the Israelites charged straight into the town and captured it"* (Joshua 6:20).

Faith can look foolish, but it opens rivers and brings walls down. It unleashes what only God can do. Joshua moved forward, endured seven years of conquest, and faced thirty armies more powerful than his. But he kept a true perspective. When Joshua looked through his telescope with the lens of faith, he saw the armed warriors perched behind their walled cities like grasshoppers. Because that is how the Commander of the Lord's army saw them.

HARD EVIDENCE IN STONE

The conquest of Canaan began with Jericho and ended with Hazor. Hazor was at one time the capital of the Northern Kingdom of Israel. It was situated on the top of a very high tel, a hill created by civilizations continually rebuilding in the same place over many years. Its walls were impressive and formidable.

Early one morning, I climbed to the top of Hazor's tel and explored the ruins. The sun was just rising and casting a golden glow over the stones of the site. Every rock told a story from the ancient past. The first thing that impressed me was the height of the hill upon which Hazor rested. But even more striking was what Joshua must have thought when he marched with his army north from the Sea of Galilee, rounded the bend in the ancient road, and was arrested by the sight of Hazor. He must have mentally retraced his steps to that night outside Jericho when he was arrested by the sight of the heavenly warrior. He must have affirmed the divine perspective, that relative to anything, God is bigger.

Joshua encountered the wall of Hazor with a direct attack. *"The Israelites completely destroyed every living thing in the city … And then Joshua burned the city"* (Joshua 11:11). That morning, as I explored the ruins of Hazor, I noted a layer of black limestone embedded in the ruins, indicating a flaming destruction at some point in history. I discovered an archeological marker stating that the presence of the black stones dated back to the time of Joshua when the walls were destroyed by fire. There it was. The ancient piles of burnt debris are the record of what happened, true to Scripture, the evidence that God is bigger.

WITNESSING THE UNEXPECTED

There was a small town tucked into the hill just over the Mount of Olives from the city of Jerusalem. Bethany. Jesus had best friends who lived here, and He frequented this town whenever He visited

Jerusalem. It was a quiet getaway after a busy day in the bustling streets of Jerusalem.

On this day, however, things were not quiet in the small town of Bethany. Everyone knew everything about everyone. News travelled by word of mouth faster than text messaging. Lazarus, one of Jesus' best friends, was very sick and seemed to be getting progressively worse. His sisters, Mary and Martha, decided it was serious enough to send for Jesus. A runner was dispatched immediately.

When Jesus received the news, He didn't seem disturbed. In fact, he delayed for two days before deciding to head out for Bethany. In the meantime, Lazarus died. What a tragedy! It didn't have to happen. Where was Jesus? Couldn't He have prevented this? Couldn't He have come and healed Lazarus? The one time they needed Jesus, and He wasn't around. He didn't show up! Ever felt that way?

On the way to Bethany, Jesus explained to the disciples that Lazarus was dead and then said something rather odd. *"For your sakes, I'm glad I wasn't there, for now you will really believe"* (John 11:15). You see, for man, death is our greatest enemy, our highest wall. For God, death is the greatest opportunity to glorify Himself and to stretch our faith in Him. Man was expecting a healing. Jesus was thinking something else.

When Jesus neared Bethany, Martha, Lazarus' sister and Jesus' good friend, raced to meet Him. She cried, *"Lord, if only you had been here"* (11:21). If you had been here. Her brother was dead. It was too late. Her perceived need was greater than her perceived resource. Her wall was greater than her God. Her perspective was faulty.

When we hit walls in our lives, "if only" sentences monopolize our thoughts. If only you had been here. If only I had been raised in a functional, loving home. If only I had found Mr. Right. If only I was healed. If only we had a child. If only I had more money. If only God would show us what is around the next bend. If only God provided. If only …

My son and daughter-in-law, Jeremy and Bonnie, have been on a faith journey. They sold their home and were in the process of buying a new home. They hadn't found one and time was running out. You know—closing dates, packing, planning. They had been riding the roller coaster, up one day and down the next. Lots of frustration and disappointment. It would have been so much easier if only God had somehow sketched out a rough draft or charted the course for them. How many times have you felt the same way? They recently said to me that it was so difficult when you didn't know what was around the next bend. I know. We've been there. You feel very insecure. Out on a limb. But, come to think of it, isn't it out on the limb where the fruit of faith grows?

I reminded them to keep their eyes on the memory aid just across the street from their present home. A little cottage-like house that I will tell you about in the next chapter. A temporary home God gave to us twenty-five years earlier in response to our need. A memory aid that still reminds us that God is present and involved in our lives, even when the clock ticks down to the last hour. It was part of our faith journey. Every follower of Jesus is on a faith journey. If you knew what was around the next bend of that journey, you wouldn't need faith, and you wouldn't grow in faith. Faith says, "I don't know what lies around the bend in the road. But He does. So I will keep my eyes off the bend and centred on Him." (This, of course, does not apply when driving down a winding mountain road.)

I have watched blossoms of the fruit of faith budding on the branches of Jeremy and Bonnie's lives as they have journeyed along. They have compared themselves to baby birds that, even before they can see, open their mouths wide out of need and in expectation that Mom will fill them. Perhaps you've watched baby birds opening their mouths to be fed. Their scrawny little bodies retreat behind wide-open, super-sized mouths. That's good, solid faith: acting while you still can't see with physical eyes and before God has provided, in anticipation that God will provide. While I was writing this chapter, Bonnie e-mailed us. "I packed a box today believing that God has asked us to start packing in preparation for His blessing. It is so good. I want to cry. Just wanted to share His goodness in this part of our journey."

Amazingly, just two weeks before their closing date, God provided a home into which they could move immediately. The entire time, their house was sitting there, empty, just waiting for God's timing. God's remarkable provision in God's perfect timing. Yes, that's what was around the next bend. There will be many more bends in the road. The faith journey continues.

You've heard the old saying, "Where God guides, He provides." Ultimately, He does provide. But usually not initially. Without faith it is impossible to please God. Therefore God is always leading us to places that stretch and build our faith. There is no faith in saying, "God has provided and therefore…" We can see the provision, right in front of us. That's sight, not faith. But there is faith in saying, "God will provide and therefore…" Craig Groeschel wrote,

> God often guides by what He doesn't provide … Are you up against a wall with no good plan to get past it? Have you hit an obstacle that appears impenetrable? Maybe God will guide you to see something that you couldn't have seen if he'd just removed the wall.[2]

Maybe you would not have received God's full blessing if He had just healed you. Maybe you would not have seen what God really wanted you to see if He had just provided the financial resources.

Groeschel continued, "If you don't have something you think you need, maybe it's because God wants you to see something you've never seen."[3] Mary and Martha were thinking a healing. Jesus was thinking a resurrection. He had hinted at this when He said, *"I am the resurrection and the life"* (John 11:25). The sisters were thinking of a visitation as they led Jesus out to where Lazarus had been entombed. Jesus was thinking of a display of God's power and glory. He felt the pain of death and wept at the graveside, but He planned to use the wall of death as a means to draw His disciples and Mary and Martha out of their familiar boxes.

Faith steps outside the familiar. It steps into the unfamiliar, the new, the fresh, to what is obviously of God, from God, because of God, full of God, and for God's glory. Jesus clearly articulated that this wall of death, the greatest wall that confronts all of us, would be used to manifest God's glory and to increase and strengthen the faith of those standing there. He shouted, *"Lazarus, come out!"* (11:43). There was a stir inside the tomb. Suddenly the opening to the grave was obstructed by the figure of a man—wrapped head, hands, and feet in grave clothes. The onlookers stood back, stunned and numb. They had just witnessed something they had never seen before or expected. They had expected Jesus to inject life into a sick man. But they had just now seen Jesus inject life into a dead man. There Lazarus was, alive. Standing before the Master over death, and the Master of life. The living proof that no matter what wall you hit, Jesus is still the Master.

Jesus proved it again by His own resurrection. Three days after His crucifixion, He rose from the dead. That was the greatest miracle ever, the miracle that changed everything. A resurrection compels you to think big, because a resurrection defies natural law. A resurrection defies human logic. A resurrection puts the wall that you hit in perspective, because relative to anything, God is bigger.

I like the way that Mark Driscoll ends his book *Vintage Church*: "Jesus is alive, anything can happen."[4]

Hold that perspective!

Cheryl's Story

DURING MY TEENAGE YEARS, I WAS SURE I HAD IT ALL FIGURED OUT. Our home was not a happy one. I would describe my dad as an unpredictable rageaholic. I decided, with God's help, I would provide a pain-free childhood for my children and ensure a great life for them. I intentionally sought a kind, predictable, loving husband so that my children would feel confident, valued, and secure with the love of a good father. This security would pave the way for making wise decisions as they grew up. Basically, I thought I could manoeuvre the course of their lives. Our home would be happy and loving without the baggage my brother and I had been saddled with. I poured myself intentionally and liberally into having the "perfect" family.

We had three children. For our older daughter, it was the second week of grade 9. Abruptly, life for my once-cheery daughter and our family took a sharp downward spiral. Jenn became gloomy and withdrawn, skipped classes, and dressed in dark clothing. We pulled and coerced her to go to numerous counselling sessions. We tried to affirm her over and over, but she continued to retreat, closing herself off from us. A cloud settled over our family that refused to lift.

We tried many ways to induce change. We changed schools. We went on a family vacation. Jenn spent the entire week of vacation in her room, isolating herself. This was followed by a short reprieve, but the peace was soon shattered. My suspicion was affirmed and my worst fears realized. My fifteen-year-old was expecting. She informed us that she had been raped. Her sense of self-worth was decimated. My husband and I resolved that we would support her in practical ways and help her work through the emotional, physical, and spiritual issues caused by these injuries.

Jenn chose to bring her baby daughter home and be a sixteen-year-old parent. She began to raise baby Sarah, but her good intentions were short lived. Things did not go well, and we had to step in almost immediately. Jenn returned to her crazy, chaotic lifestyle. She was soon pregnant again and just twelve months after the birth of Sarah, gave birth to a new little one. This time Jenn chose an adoptive family. I genuinely thought that we would begin again as a family. Such was not to be. Chaos reigned.

Jenn's irresponsible behaviour was so affecting her young daughter and her thirteen-year-old sister that we were compelled to tell her to leave until she decided to change. Angry, she left but took Sarah with her to a drug/party house. We spent a gruelling three days on a rescue mission for the baby. We recognized the need to have custody of little Sarah and began the painful process of battling with our daughter for the custody of her baby. We eventually got custody and, in fact, later adopted Sarah.

In those interim years, Jenn had no fixed address. She was sometimes living with a boyfriend. She continued on drugs. She had supervised visits with Sarah. There were often "no-shows." It was difficult to show tough love with our teen child. But her continuing negative influence was so impacting the family, including our concern for the safety and welfare of everyone, that we needed to maintain boundaries even though we knew that the boundaries added to her pain.

We received the news again. The arrival of baby three… then baby four. All born before Jenn was twenty years old. Both infants were placed in different homes. We may never see them again. I cried out to God. "What about my goal for an almost pain-free childhood for my children? What about my desire to provide them with a good life?" Too many walls!

As I write this, Jenn has given birth to two more children, and she is raising them in an unpredictable life out of province. Our now teenage daughter Sarah is doing fairly well. She suffers from deep wounds of abandonment and loss. Jenn appears and disappears in and out of our lives. She exhibits a love/hate relationship with us. We all have wounds, injury, and baggage. Clearly, I wasn't able to control my children's lives.

My heart aches for my daughter.

7

Waiting at the Wall

YOU'VE HEARD THOSE UNWELCOME WORDS, "YOU'LL HAVE TO WAIT, ma'am." "You'll have to wait, sir." They are on the same base level as those ominous words that proceed from the mouth of your dentist as he pulls up his chair close to your defenseless head with that big needle in his hand. "Open your mouth. Please open your mouth. This won't hurt." It's the same with waiting. Waiting is not a welcome word. Waiting is not easy. Never has been. Maybe that's why God says over and over again, "Wait on the Lord."

The grocery store is a place where you can learn a lot about waiting. You stroll into the store, find a cart without wobbly wheels that steers straight, casually look around for any booths with free food samples being handed out, make your way up and down the aisles looking for the food items you need, and, just before you go, make the rounds again to the booths with free samples hoping that by now the distributor with the apron doesn't recognize that this is your second time around—or third. Then comes the time of testing. Tension. The lineup at the checkout! You take a quick, discerning scan over the lines. You then make a hurried judgment about which line to move toward. You need to mentally calculate numerous factors. The length of the line. The quantity of items in each cart in the line. The speed of the cashier in moving things through the line. The distance from your present position to the line. The number of competitors potentially rivaling you for your spot in the line. And the number of carts you'll need to dodge getting to the line ahead of your nearest contender.

I have discovered two laws of waiting. They are as certain as the law of gravity. The first is the law of progress. When a line is making good progress, the person in front of you will need a price check! The second is the law of line length. The shortest line takes the longest time! So get used to waiting. Just when you think you've figured it out, you haven't.

A friend of mine told me a story of when he recently took his daughter out for a father-daughter time to a baseball game. They decided to line up at the hotdog stand before entering the dome. They waited in line patiently for about a half hour. The game began. They could hear the crowd cheering. They were still in line. Just as it was their turn to order their hotdogs, a beautiful looking woman ran up to him, threw her arms around him, cried that she hadn't seen him for such a long time, and gave him a big kiss on the lips. He stood there, dazzled by her beauty, bewildered as to who she was, and confused by how he should know her. But then, when he finally came to, he realized with a dumbfounded sense of stupidity that he had been duped. He watched her as she ran off with two hotdogs in her hands.

Some time ago, the following verse was sent to us from a friend at a time when we were learning (or should I say struggling?) to wait. The words arrived like a letter from heaven.

> When everything is pleasant and bright,
> And the things we do turn out just right,
> We feel without question that God is real,
> For, when we are happy, how good we feel.
> But when the tide turns and gone is the song,
> And misfortune comes and our plans go wrong,
> Doubt creeps in and we start to wonder,
> Our thoughts about God are torn asunder.
> For we feel deserted in times of deep stress,
> Without God's presence to assure us and bless.
> It's then when our feelings and senses are reeling,
> We realize clearly it's faith and not feeling—

For it takes true faith to patiently wait,
Believing God comes not too soon or too late.[1]

In a previous chapter I conveyed that a major component of the wall we hit was the stress of having to move six times in one year. As I journaled through that year, I continually used the word *wait*. And it didn't seem to be getting easier. Vicky forwarded the words above to us in the midst of that struggle. In fact, on the same day that we put out our fleece.

OUR MIRACLE HOME

One month later, and after one more move, we had the assurance that God had led us to the town of Aurora to serve Him there. In a remarkable way, He provided a home we knew was from Him for us. We were elated. There was one problem. The closing date was three months away—August 31st. The house we were living in had been sold, and the closing date was eight days ahead. We had to be out! We needed to find a place to live for the interim. A wrinkle; well, more than a wrinkle. Find a place today. Be able to move into that place within the week. And find a landlord who would agree to us living there for only three months. Every step forward seemed to be followed by another step backward. We seemed to be always waiting: waiting for the phone to ring, waiting for someone to get back to us, waiting to just land! We felt like a plane running out of fuel, losing altitude, while circling round and round, looking for a place to set down before we crashed.

Mindful of the fact that we had to have our family out of our present home in eight days, Diane and I drove to Aurora early the next morning to search for a rental house. We prayed every mile of the way with the pressure of "eight days" gnawing away at our peace. The last line of Vicky's poem kept coming back to me. "God comes not too soon or too late." The Spirit spoke to me in a quiet, reassuring way. "You trust and wait, and I'll provide, right on time."

There were only two places for rent that we could find in the newspaper. We inquired into both and struck out both times. I was a batter coming to the plate with two down and needing a home run, and the owner of the second house pitched me another ball. As we were returning to our car, he gave me the phone number of a friend who wanted to rent a house. He had seen the notice posted at work. I phoned his friend and shared our need.

He informed me that he was in real estate part-time and that he had sold a small house to an elderly lady. Her plans were to move into the house in the near future. While we sat in his office, he made a phone call to the lady. When he put the phone down, he smiled and said we could move into the house today. She planned to move into the house in September and would be happy to rent it to us for three months until August 31st. Home run! God had come not too soon or too late. We had the house for exactly the time we needed.

Several days later, we were moving our boxes into our miracle home. It was a pocket-sized house, but it was sufficient. It was God's provision. It was heaven to us. Our generous landlady even renovated the kitchen and the tiny bathroom. For several days, while our kitchen and bathroom were out of order, we would round the kids up and head down to McDonalds several times a day for hamburgers and bathroom breaks. It was an adventure. That summer, I pastored our small church. My study, our everything, was in that small home. It was our Brook Cherith. We drank from its waters and watched God provide our daily bread in incredible ways.

At the end of our stay, August 31st, we moved into our new home we had purchased several months earlier. A week later, I was driving past our little miracle home, and I noticed a for-sale sign on the lawn. I was surprised. I looked into it, and as it turned out, the elderly lady had decided not to relocate and was trying to sell the house. It was as though God had told her to purchase that house for us for three months, renovate and refresh the kitchen and bathroom, and then sell it after we had gone.

We will never forget that house. It's the house I referred to in the previous chapter, just across the street from the home of my son and daughter-in-law. Every time we drive by it, we are refreshingly reminded of God's provision and of our need to wait on Him and trust Him. It is something I don't ever want to lose. I don't think waiting ever gets easy.

But it yields gratifying reward and unleashes divine purpose and value, for it carries with it God's wonderful daily provision and sometimes miraculous intervention.

BEAUTIFUL IN HIS TIME

I have been moved at the Wailing Wall in old Jerusalem. The wall is all that remains of the temple of Jesus' day after its destruction by the Romans in 70 AD. The temple once sparkled like a jewel on Mount Zion, having been beautified by Herod the Great. The huge stones of the Wailing Wall stand as the last vestige of a once-magnificent structure, a memorial to past glory, a reminder of dashed hopes and aspirations, and a symbol of future hope and dreams. Worshippers approach the wall with their shawls wrapped around their heads, phylacteries strapped to their arms, and place small, rolled-up pieces of paper between the cracks of the venerable stones. It is a time to pray. And wail. And wait. Wait for God to restore. Wait for God to fulfill His promises.

When you come to any wall in your life, you will discover that it is a time to wait. You unfold and spread out before God your pain and longings and pray… and wait … and pray … and wait. Hard waits. A childless couple waiting for a child. An elderly and sick man waiting to die and go to be with Jesus in heaven. A single woman waiting to find the right spouse. A lonely person waiting to find a friend with a kindred spirit. A spouse waiting for a gentle and understanding word. A patient waiting for a diagnosis.

Waiting is one of the consistent themes in the Bible. Isaiah wrote, *"Those who trust in the LORD will find new strength. They will soar high on wings like eagles. They will run and not grow weary. They will walk and not faint"* (Isaiah 40:31). To trust in the Lord embraces waiting for the Lord. The psalmist penned out of his own personal experience: *"Wait patiently for the LORD. Be brave and courageous. Yes, wait patiently for the LORD"* (Psalm 27:14). Abraham and Sarah waited twenty-five years at the wall for their promised son, Isaac. Hannah waited at the wall of infertility for many years, enduring ridicule from wife number two. David was anointed as king by Samuel and won a stunning victory over the giant Goliath. He then waited thirteen years before actually becoming king, forced to flee and hide in the wilderness of Judea. Joseph was seventeen years old when he was betrayed by his own brothers and separated from his father. God's dreams were fulfilled for Joseph's life in God's time. But not before thirteen years of slavery and imprisonment. And it was about twenty-two years before he ever saw his family again. Sometimes our prayers seem to accumulate like unopened letters on the table of an absent friend. But the discipline of delay is one of the ways of God. And He makes all things beautiful in His time.

A SONG ABOUT WAITING

Why has God established the discipline of waiting? Psalm 37 is about waiting, and it gives us some keys to unlocking our understanding of why. David was struggling with the prosperity of evil people and conversely the adversity of righteous people. David was very familiar with this problem from personal experience. As David worked his way through these perplexing issues, he reduced his contemplations and reflections to some essential truths. These truths unlock the "why" for waiting. They blend together, inseparable.

David stated that if you delight in the presence of the Lord, "He *will give you your heart's desires*" (37:4, emphasis added). Then in verse 5, he urges you to commit everything to the Lord's control, for you can be assured that "He *will help you.*" "He *will make your innocence radiate like the dawn, and the justice of your cause will shine like the noonday sun*" (37:6, emphasis added). Note the progression of time from the dawn to noonday. It takes time, but His purposes come together. Waiting unravels any illusion that you are in control of your life and focuses on His control and timing. *"We are God's masterpiece"* (Ephesians 2:10). Think of it. God is creating a masterpiece. He is writing the script. He is assembling the pieces. He is fashioning the shape of your life. He is building the structure. He is the Potter, and you are the clay. You are all about Him. The purpose for your life is wrapped up in His purposes. He is in control.

When David was hiding out in the wilderness from the treacherous King Saul, he had two great opportunities to take Saul's life. On the first occasion, Saul walked into the very cave where David and his men were hiding out, to make a pit stop (1 Samuel 24). On the second occasion, David slipped past the guards into Saul's camp at night (1 Samuel 26). He got right up to where Saul was sleeping. But he refused to take things into his own hands. Instead, he took Saul's spear and water jug. It was as though God had handed Saul into David's hands. Both times were David's opportunities to remove the obstacle, escape from this wilderness living, and jump headlong into the kingship. After all, wasn't that where God was taking him? But David chose discerningly to spare Saul's life and leave his own life in God's hands, to His timing, under His control. When David finally became king, he wanted to have the assurance that he was where he was because God had put him there. Waiting has a way of giving you the same assurance.

Waiting also gives you a greater capacity for God. Read through Psalm 37 and note the number of times and the number of ways that David articulated the greatness of God, evidenced in His help, presence, power, care, provision, guidance, faithfulness. It is natural for us to be narrow in our life focus. To become preoccupied with our personal needs and wants. To centre on our own hurts and struggles. Waiting at the wall gives you an opportunity to increase your knowledge of God and His ways. Psalm 103:7 tells us that God revealed His ways to Moses and His deeds to the people of Israel. The Hebrew word for "way" refers to the road God is taking. There is a difference between the deeds of God and the ways of God. Anyone can see the deeds of God. Understanding His ways—the path God takes, the way He does things—goes much deeper. Waiting at the wall is perhaps the primal way that God takes us deeper. Waiting teaches you that God's goal is not the removal of the wall, but the use of the wall to restore one's preoccupation with Him. It was at the wall where David learned to *"delight in the Lord"* (Psalm 37:4). God's purpose is for us to know Him and to enjoy His intimate presence and friendship (37:4). And to be still in His presence (37:7).

TRUSTING AND CAREFREE

Psalm 37 unfolds a third truth for unlocking the "why" for waiting. It is a psalm about waiting and trusting. Waiting and trusting are conjoined twins. The purpose of waiting is to learn to trust God in everything. Trust, or you can call it faith, is so important to God that it is impossible to please Him without it. Faith is what links you to Him. Faith lies at the root of relationship with Him. God will do whatever it takes to strengthen and deepen faith. Psalm 37 begins, *"Don't worry … or envy … [but] trust in the LORD"* (verses 1–3). The Hebrew word for "trust," as used here, means to be so confident that you can be carefree. You are so taken care of that there is no need for you to worry or carry any burden or care. You can confidently *"give all your worries and cares to God, for he cares about … you"* (1 Peter 5:7). You do the casting; He will do the caring. You are carefree. Take some time just to meditate on that truth. Waiting will begin to take on new meaning.

In Psalm 37:5, David emphasizes the need to commit everything. *Commit* means to "roll upon." You fall into bed dog-tired. You roll your tired body and mind—with all of your cares and burdens—upon your bed, entrusting yourself to it, and fall sound asleep. It is the same word that's used in Psalm 22:8: *"Is this the one who* relies *on the LORD? Then let the LORD save him!"* (emphasis added). It was this phrase that Jesus' mockers threw back at Him when He was dying on the cross. *"He trusted God, so let God rescue him now"* (Matthew 27:43). At His darkest moment, Jesus "rolled upon" His Father and entrusted Himself completely to His care. If Jesus needed to do that, how much more do we? Too often we are like the man riding his horse while carrying a heavy burden on his back. You ask him, "Why don't you remove that heavy burden from your back and lay it on the back of the horse?" He replies, "Why, I prefer to keep it on my shoulders so as to keep the weight off of the horse." Funny, until we realize that's what we do. Then it's not so funny. We say we entrust our lives to God, and then we carry our burdens.

DEPENDING

I checked *Webster's Dictionary* for the meaning of the word *trust*. It means to "depend." So I checked the word *depend*. Interestingly, *depend* comes from the Latin word *pendere*. Suddenly, my four years of high school Latin bore some fruit. *Pendere* is a verb meaning "to hang." *Webster's* gives the meaning for depend as, "existing by virtue of a necessary relation." It all came together for me. One's existence hangs from the necessary existence of another. A child exists by virtue of a necessary relationship to the parent. The child needs the parent to exist. I exist by virtue of God. I need Him to exist. I exist in absolute dependence upon Him, whether I realize it or not.

But taking it to the next level, the quality of my existence is determined by the quality and excellence of my relationship with God. And the quality of my relationship with God is governed by the degree to which I am aware that He is an absolute necessity. Recognizing my absolute reliance on Him. Living my life in absolute dependence on Him. God desires to cultivate in our lives the deepest possible relationship with Himself. So He cultivates our dependence on Him. And His way to cultivate dependence is to allow circumstances in life that bring us to the end of ourselves. We are left *hanging*.

HANGING BY A ROPE

Let me share three word pictures. It is said a picture is worth a thousand words. All three pictures espouse the concept of hanging. You may not remember all three. But try to carry one of them away. It will help you understand what it means to trust in God and to depend on Him. One night, as I watched the news on television, I was intrigued by the story of an attempted rescue of a man from a burning high-rise. The man was leaning out of the window, trying to get up the nerve to jump and end his life quickly rather than fall prey to the rapacious flames. Several firefighters suddenly appeared on the roof of the towering building directly above the panicking man. They acted with quick deliberation. One of the firemen began to tie a rope under his arms while the others secured the other end of the rope to their waists. The first rescuer then rolled to his stomach and dropped both legs over the edge of the building. The other rescuers braced themselves as they began to lower his body precariously down over the side. They moved him slowly but steadily in the direction of their intended target, the panic-stricken man. After several minutes the rescue was complete and successful.

Put yourself in the place of the lone rescuer hanging over the edge of that towering building. You need to believe in the strength of the rope and the strength of the ones anchoring it. You are hanging, depending. It may seem as though you've been waiting forever. But you are held by the rope of God. It won't break. And God anchors it. He holds you, and He won't let go. You rely. That's trust! That's relationship with the true God.

HANGING FROM THE RAFTERS

The second word picture comes from a book I read many years ago. *Bruchko* is the story of a young man, Bruce Olson, who left home and travelled to the jungles of South America to take the good news about Jesus to the Motilones, a murderous tribe of headhunters. It is an amazing story that will keep you on the edge of your seat until you finish the book. Among the many things Olson accomplished among the Motilones was reducing their language to writing, and translating several New Testament books into the Motilone language.

Some words were difficult to translate in a way the Motilone would understand. One such word was *faith*. The meaning of the word dawned on Bruce one day as he lay in his hammock. The Motilone tied their hammocks high in the rafters of their communal homes. Bruce was afraid to climb into the high hammocks for fear that the strings would break and he would plummet to the ground. He wanted his hammock tied low so he could have one foot in the hammock and one foot on the floor. The Motilone would laugh and tell him he had to place both feet in the hammock and be suspended to truly rest.[2] Suspend. There's another *pendere* word. *Webster's* defines *suspend* in this way: "to hang as to be free on all sides except at the point of support." Bruce had found the key to unlocking the meaning of faith. Faith is tying your hammock strings into Jesus Christ and resting while suspended in God. The Motilone would describe accepting Jesus into their lives as "tying their hammock strings into Jesus."[3]

What a great picture of what it means to trust God. Tie the strings of your life into Christ. Place both feet inside the hammock. Sometimes, it may seem like you're hanging by only a thread. But rest with no fear of falling. You are hanging free from all cares on all sides. You are secure because you are tied at the point of support, which is God. That's the point the psalmist reached when he penned, *"Be still in the presence of the LORD"* (Psalm 37:7).

HANGING IN MIDAIR

The third picture comes from the well-known priest and writer Henri Nouwen, who wrote much about the spiritual life. Nouwen had become good friends with a family of trapeze artists, the Flying Rodleighs. Most of us have at some point in our lives been to a circus and watched with rapt fascination the man on the flying trapeze. There is a flyer and a catcher. Both grip a trapeze with their strong hands and begin to swing. The two trapeze artists sway back and forth, back and forth, putting their full energy into getting a strong upward lift. It is more like a dance as they swing rhythmically past each other, barely missing. Nouwen explained that there has to be a good relationship between the flyer and the catcher.[4] That may be an understatement. After all, the life of the flyer will literally be placed in the hands of the catcher.

Suddenly, on one of those upward sweeps, the flyer lets go of the trapeze. His body takes upward flight like an arrow until it stops in midair. Frozen in space. Arms extended. Suspended in weightlessness. Like a still photo. Waiting. The trapeze is gone. He can't press rewind or fast forward. He is stuck on pause. Now is not the time to panic, even though there is no evidence, no indication of the catcher. Rodleigh told Nouwen that the flyer "must wait in absolute trust."[5] It seems like forever, but it's only a second. At just the right time, the hands of the catcher snatch him.

While the psalmist did not have a trapeze artist in mind, I can visualize this picture when I read Psalm 37. Verse 5 says to commit everything to the Lord. Let go of the trapeze. There are things God tells you to release. So let go. And hang. Suspended. Waiting. You feel vulnerable and exposed. Don't panic. The psalmist begs you, *"Be still"* (37:7). You may not feel or see God's presence. But the Catcher is close by. *"Wait patiently for him to act"* (37:7). Wait in absolute confidence that He'll catch you. He will not be a second too early. Not a second too late. In His perfect timing, He will catch you. Your relationship with the Catcher assures you that you can trust Him.

Sharon's Story

I HUNG UP THE TELEPHONE. IT HAD BEEN MY DOCTOR. HE WANTED TO see us right away as something was wrong with the pregnancy. That's all he said. I felt unnerved. Alarmed. My mind began to run in all directions. My husband was at work. I called my sister-in-law and when she answered her phone, I just sobbed.

The next day, my husband and I went down to the doctor's office. I wanted to know. I didn't want to know. His explanation of what was wrong was brief and to the point. Our unborn baby had spina bifida. The baby could be born paralyzed, mentally disabled, or even die. We left the office with very heavy hearts.

Even before Ben was born, he struggled to survive. Before he was two weeks old, he had undergone two surgeries. We had to learn how to care for him on our own. A sense of physical exhaustion and emotional drain always threatened. The days turned into months of information overload. Doctor's appointments. Multiple surgeries. Financial strain. Trying to access financial assistance, feeling like we had to plead for every penny. Emergency crises. Fear. Will Ben make it this time? Will he be the same if he does pull through?

We often felt guilt regarding our other two sons. Did they feel neglected because Mom and Dad's energies were so focused on Ben? We regularly felt misunderstood by people and wanted to withdraw. We chronically looked at Ben and wondered how long he would be with us. We wanted to hold on to him tightly and provide him with the best quality of life while every day was a challenge, both as a parent and a caregiver, helping him to survive.

There are days when I wake up, my feet hit the floor, and I am running again. Always loving. Always learning. Sometimes overwhelmed. But determined to keep going.

8 Persevering at the Wall

On April 16, 2007, tragedy struck the town of Blacksburg, Virginia. Blacksburg is home to the renowned university Virginia Tech. Its old, historical stone buildings beautifully adorn the middle of town. On that fateful day, an armed gunman entered one of the main buildings at Virginia Tech and opened fire, killing thirty-two people. It was the deadliest peacetime shooting to date by a single gunman in U.S. history. Today, there is a monument on the university grounds where one can stroll past thirty-two memorial stones dedicated to the memory and name of each person killed. One is poignantly touched by the notes and letters expressing grief, loss, friendship, and remembrance laid beside each name.

This was not the first massacre to occur on these grounds. Another had happened two hundred and fifty years earlier. This was actually the primary reason Diane and I had come to Blacksburg. I love history. I have enjoyed it since I was a child. I love to read about people who have lived before us, their exploits, adventures, hardships, and ways. And then, I am motivated to set out and find the places and landmarks significant to their lives. This magnetic curiosity inspires me. I have come to recognize that with this interest, there is so much to learn from what has gone before. I think that to understand who we are and where we are going, we need to better understand where we have come from. I believe that to fully appreciate each other with all of our unique differences, we would serve ourselves well to better understand how we all fit together from an historical perspective. And I have discovered that the characters of those who have lived in times past are a wonderful source of inspiration for our lives today.

Well, I was on another historical quest to research a story that had interested me for some time and to discover some of its significant places. Diane, my wife, has always enjoyed coming along. While I am wading through some swamp or rummaging through some old building, she will be in the car enjoying a good book. Sometimes, in fact, the story will draw her into its hold, and she will become personally interested and engaged. This became one of those cases. The story entailed the life and experiences of Mary Draper Ingles. Her name became familiar in the best-selling novel *Follow the River* by Alexander Thom.

When we arrived at Virginia Tech, I looked up a local historian to give me an historical perspective of the narrative from someone on location. She made the interesting comment that when the most recent massacre occurred, some questioned whether or not this tract of land might be cursed ground. She then added that, interestingly, the account of the first massacre became a source of inspiration and hope to much of the university's faculty and student body in the aftermath of the second. A story has great power to influence and inspire.

THE LONG WAY HOME

The Duck Pond is a peaceful spot on the campus of Virginia Tech. On a warm spring day, you will find students sprawled on the grass reading and studying. Two hundred and fifty years ago, this same spot was a marshy area with a quiet meadow and bubbling stream flowing through it. This was the location of a small settlement on the edge of the frontier. Drapers Meadows. The Drapers were some of the original settlers who had come west through the Appalachians to find a new life. Mary Draper was a strong, youthful frontier woman who caught the eye of a young, hardworking man, William Ingles. Their marriage was the first white wedding west of the Alleghenies. They began to carve out of the wilderness a space for themselves and welcomed two sons into their family, Thomas and George.

The French and Indian War had just begun, and hostilities and bloodshed were beginning to escalate across the western frontier. Native peoples allied to the French were attacking British settlements, burning them to the ground. Retaliations were becoming commonplace. A half-buried stone marker at the Duck Pond on the university campus gives faint indication to what happened one warm Sunday morning at Drapers Meadows on July 30, 1755. The men were out working in the fields while the women were busily engaged with the grinding tasks of settlement life. Children were playing between the cabins. Suddenly, Shawnee warriors appeared from the margins of the forest and swooped in upon the unsuspecting settlement of scattered cabins. Cries went up as settlers met certain and brutal death. The men heard the desperate screams, grabbed their guns, and came running. But before they arrived, the bloodshed was done, and the Shawnee had fled with five hostages. Among them, twenty-three-year-old Mary Ingles and her two sons, Thomas (four years old) and George (two years old).

They were led hastily along the New River gorge. Conditions were grim and fright gripped the hostages, who were still in a state of shock. Some accounts say Mary was nine months pregnant. Several days into the flight, Mary gave birth to a little daughter. She was sent into the bushes to give birth and then ordered back onto her horse with her newborn and told to keep riding. Mary guarded her two sons like a mother bear, while trying not to provoke her captors. She kept an eye on one of the other hostages, her sister-in-law, who was being more harshly treated by the Shawnee. Mary refused to show any cowardice or timidity. She encouraged and consoled. She was determined to survive and to keep her sons alive. She worked hard making salt and sewing shirts for her assailants. In fact, her strong determination, courage, and grit fostered a sense of respect and admiration from her captors that served to spare her from running the gauntlet and earned her favour and approval.

The hostages were led down the New River, along the Kanawha, and finally down the mighty Ohio River to a large Indian village. It was frightening to enter a village amidst people yelling taunts and insults and without any knowledge of what was going to happen next. To Mary's horror, her sons were separated from her and taken away. She would never see young George again. Thomas would vanish for thirteen years. Her fear and panic was checked only by her persevering sense of survival. Mary was taken farther west along the Ohio River, farther than any white woman had ever been.

Mary had paid close attention to the route followed by the Shawnee. Deprived of her two sons, she resolved to escape and return to her husband William. Death in the wilderness would be better than slavery in the hands of the Shawnee. Hence plans were hatched for one of the greatest escapes of all time. She shared her plans with one other hostage, described only as an "old Duch [Dutch] woman."[1] The older woman agreed to go with her. One day, while out picking berries, the two women made their getaway.

Mary knew her only chance of a successful return was to follow the rivers. They were the path home. This was the beginning of a long and arduous journey, thought impossible by anyone except Mary. Exposure. Hunger. Innumerable setbacks. Wild animals. Bruised and bleeding bodies. Their clothes became tattered and their shoes worn out. They endured cold nights and snow. At night they would curl up in a hollow log and cover themselves with dry leaves to try and keep warm.

They could not drift on a log or raft since they were travelling against the current. Neither woman could swim. This meant that when they came to a tributary flowing into the river they were following, they would have to backtrack up this river until they found a place to cross. Then walk down the tributary to the mouth again. They encountered rocky ridge after rocky ridge. They pulled themselves up over the craggy ridges, sliding down the opposite sides.

John Ingles, son of Mary Ingles, later wrote an account as given to him by his mother. He wrote, "They wood attempt to cross these points of riges to shorten their distance and by being woorn down by fateigue & starvation wood have to pule themselves up by the srubs & bushes till they got to the top and to decend they wood slide all the way down Under These defiqualteys and nothing to sustain nature but what they picked up in the woods such as black walnuts grapes pawpaws etc. & very often so pushed with hunger that they wood dig up roots & eate that they knew nothing of."[2]

They finally reached the New River gorge. The Indians called it the river of death. The trek was becoming more and more exhausting with every step. They were like dead women walking. The old Dutch woman was becoming increasingly unpleasant. One day she attacked Mary, who barely escaped with her life. Mary took flight along the river. She discovered an old canoe buried in the river bank which she used to paddle herself to the other side of the river.

Thirty miles from home she was confronted by the greatest wall of rock yet encountered. Anvil Rock. The precipice descended right down into the fast-moving river. Mary tried to wade around it, but to no avail. She faced the inevitable. A momentous climb over the face of the steep rock. I remember the day I located Anvil Rock. The cliffs rise into the sky like mighty palisades defying anyone to pass. Today, a set of railroad tracks line the base of the cliff. I followed the tracks back to the place where Mary must have begun her ascent.

She defied the wall. She climbed, pulling herself up by the roots of shrubs, resting occasionally to reserve what little strength remained in her. Two days. That's how long it took her to claw her way up and over the top. She rolled down the other side and out into a small clearing where she collapsed, exhausted. She was found by hunters. She was twenty-three years old. Her hair had turned white. She was naked, skeletal, bloodied, more dead than alive. She had walked approximately eight hundred miles in forty-two days through some of the harshest country in the frontier. One step at a time. Just to get home. But she did it!

After my experience at Anvil Rock, we travelled through the beautiful mountainous landscape of the Appalachian country. I wanted to find Ingles Ferry. After Mary's reunion with her husband William and some time to heal and recuperate from her horrendous ordeal, although she never truly recovered emotionally, William and Mary established and maintained a ferry business on the New River near Radford, Virginia. Ingles Ferry became the crossing point on the New River for the wagon trains moving westward on the Wilderness Road. On the east side of the river, William and Mary built a small log home and operated a farm. On the opposite side of the river, they built a tavern to feed and lodge weary travellers on their trek west.

As we were driving, we came upon a sign: "Ingles Farm." We drove down a narrow road to a closed gate. We eased our way past the gate toward a man out in the field. I approached him, not knowing whether he might resent my trespassing. To my surprise, he was a very warm and inviting man. His name: Lewis Ingles Jeffries. Most people called him Bud. I had just found the great-great-great-great-grandson of Mary Ingles. He is still living in the original house built by Mary's son John Ingles. He showed us through a log house which he had built, a replica of the first log house built by William and Mary on the original foundation. It had one room with a ladder leading to an upper sleeping level. A fireplace for cooking and warmth. One small window and a single door. We toured the property where Mary had spent the rest of her life. We stood under the trees in the old cemetery at her gravesite. William died at the age of fifty-three. Mary survived him by another thirty-three years, living to eighty-three in the original homestead.

Bud told us we could roam the property and stay as long as we wanted. We walked back in time down to the river's edge. Some of the trees were gigantic. Their trunks measured twelve feet across and gave witness to watching Mary and William taking that same walk under their protective boughs two hundred and fifty years earlier. At the riverbank one could still see where the old ferry had docked.

My eyes cast across the river. The sun was setting, and the shadows of dusk were swiftly shading the west bank. There stood another log building, the white plaster between its grey logs attracting us to its lonely presence. It was the old original tavern operated by the Ingles. If you listened carefully, you could hear the sound of its voice echoing back to a time when it hosted weary travellers and hunters. Daniel Boone himself, the famed frontiersman of the same period, was said to have passed this way and stayed overnight in the tavern. It now stood forlorn and friendless. I wanted to find my way over to the west side of the river. So off we drove.

We twisted and turned our way along a winding road until we came to an abrupt stop in front of another locked gate with an ominous sign posted on it forbidding trespassers. The warning seemed a little foreboding, so I got out of the vehicle and proceeded with caution down to the riverbank to a place where I could get a decent photo looking up at the old tavern. The crack of a branch under my feet flushed a deer from its resting place. It startled me more than I startled it. I had just gotten over the scare and decided to head back to the vehicle when something else alerted me. Without warning, a voice rather brusque and commanding ordered my retreat. I turned and looked. A scruffy older-looking man stood not twenty feet from me, his hands on his hips, and a very visible firearm holstered to the side of his leg. He gave me minimal time to get off the property. I assessed the situation. It looked to me like this man was a veteran from the civil war and was still intent on keeping Yankees off the land. I quickly informed him that I was a Canadian. He said he knew. He had already checked the license plate. I found that a little unnerving.

I thought to myself that I had gotten this far. If I could befriend the stranger, maybe this could turn to my favour. I told him my name and enlightened him as to why I was here. I had come all the way from Canada because of my interest in the Mary Ingles story and my desire to see this place. I asked him his name and informed him that he might be the very key to making my trip a success (or not!). The tension broke. He gave me his name. He enlightened me as to who he was: the guardian of this historical location. His job was to keep trespassers out. I told him he was doing a good job. We became immediate friends. He invited me in. I called Diane, who approached us guardedly. He showed us the tavern. He told us the stories. He pointed out a small clearing where the wagons would circle while camped overnight. He led us a little way along the original wilderness road to a hill where the heavily loaded wagons had to be assisted with extra horse power. It was now dark. We shook hands, and I thanked him. It had been a good day.

Mary Draper Ingles. This was her story. This was the story that inspired many at the wall of their pain, grief, and loss, in the aftermath of the Virginia Tech massacre. A story of that frontier mentality which embodied tenacity, grit, hope, and perseverance.

STEADFAST ENDURANCE

The writer of Hebrews penned his book to believers in Christ who were enduring great suffering and finding it so severe they were tempted to turn back, throw in the towel, give up, quit. The writer encouraged them to remember back to earlier days. *"Think back to those early days when you first learned about Christ. Remember how you remained faithful even though it meant terrible suffering"* (10:32). The words *"remained faithful"* are the translation of the Greek verb *hupomeno*, which means to patiently endure with hope and confidence. Steadfastly endure.

It would refer to a mountain climber determined against all odds to reach the summit. The climber strives for excellence. Nothing less will prevail. The mind resists mediocrity. *Mediocrity* comes from the Latin and means "halfway up the mountain." The climber grows weary with the strain and becomes satisfied with getting halfway. A lot of people live in the mountain village of Mediocre. It can become comfortable. The view is good enough. They settle for less. The higher you go, the lonelier it becomes. The risk increases. The strain intensifies. Many don't pass the point of Mediocre. Mediocrity means to abort the struggle and to fall short of what God is doing in your life through exertion. God is doing so much in your life through the struggle of the climb if you will just keep putting one foot in front of the other. Don't fall short of the summit. Patient endurance means to keep going—just as Mary Ingles did—and refuse to quit. To reach for excellence.

Hupomeno referred to a soldier who was wounded in battle and fell to the ground. But then he pulled himself to his knees, dragged himself to his feet, staggered forward, and kept going. No matter what the enemy threw at him, he could not be stopped. He refused to quit. *Hupomeno* is not a passive word, but an active word. It doesn't mean to stand there and passively weather the storm. To just resign yourself to a hopeless plight. It means to intently get up and endure forward. Yes, you've been wounded. It would be easier to lie down and die. But you get up. Advance. Forge ahead with blazing hope. There is a life to live. Your life. A victory to claim.

The writer of Hebrews described the terrible suffering the Christians of that time period were exposed to.

> *Sometimes you were exposed to public ridicule and were beaten, and sometimes you helped others who were suffering the same*

things. You suffered along with those who were thrown into jail, and when all you owned was taken from you, you accepted it with joy (10:33–34).

There is no doubt they had hit the foreboding wall of persecution. But for everything they lost, they gained much more. Hitting the wall often draws the spirit of tenacity out of the human spirit. Hitting the wall penetrates the inner core of your being and extracts untapped resources. The painful experience stretches you beyond your perceived limits. *"Patient endurance [hupomonai] is what you need now"* (10:36). Some things never change. They needed a confident spirit of perseverance then. We need it now, today.

SEVERE ENDURANCE

The word *perseverance* comes from the Latin word *perseverus*. You readily recognize the root word *severe*. *Perseverance* means "through severity." *Perseverance* means to combat severe trials and setbacks with severe endurance. Walls have a way of threatening to consume you, but the spirit of perseverance is the same spirit, the same dogged determination, the same overcoming resolve as demonstrated by Mary Ingles to get home despite the current of everything flowing against her.

I used to have a comic hanging on my office wall that showed a frog being swallowed by a great blue heron. It seems like all is over for Mr. Frog as the heron snatches him up and prepares to gulp him down. But at just the last second, the frog makes a desperate, death-defying attempt to save himself from certain doom. With his head already in the heron's mouth, Mr. Frog flings his long wiry arms out each side of the heron's mouth and clutches the bird around its scrawny throat with his hands and holds on tenaciously. Stalemate. The frog cannot retreat. The heron cannot swallow. The heron, eyes bulging, will not release his dinner. But Mr. Frog will not let go. In big bold letters across the top of the page it says, "NEVER GIVE UP!" Looking at the grasp of that froggie, I can tell who is going to win out.

LOOKS CAN BE DECEIVING

The book of Revelation is a message from the commander-in-chief, Jesus Christ, to His troops. Things do not look good. The devil stands like a fire-breathing dragon ready to devour the church. He and his forces have launched severe strikes against the kingdom of Christ. The assault is merciless and vicious. Appearances would say the kingdom of evil is bringing the kingdom of God to its knees, which, come to think of it, is where we should be anyway. On our knees calling out to God in dependence upon Him.

Let's admit it. Who's kidding whom? We look a bit like Gideon's tattered three hundred followers heading across the Jezreel Valley armed with flashlights, ceramic jars, and whistles to take on the Midianite hordes. That's like going after the Taliban with flyswatters. Or think of David, the shepherd boy, strutting up to the hulking Goliath—who is frothing at the mouth and looks more like an armoured tank than a man—with a slingshot. But looks can be deceiving. Sometimes God allows us to run up against the menacing, sinister wall just so He can reveal His power, glory, and ability in our lives and situation.

And so the Lord Jesus sends a message to His troops. The church. You. Me. "Times are hard. Times will become increasingly harder. It will look like the devil is winning. But looks are deceiving. I am on the throne of this universe. I am in control. There will be battles. We will win some. We will lose some. But let Me reveal to you the end of the story. We will win the war. In fact, the war has already been won. Satan and evil were defeated at the cross. My cross. Victory is certain. Now you know the end of the story. So persevere until you plant the flag at the top of the hill."

Jesus opened the book of Revelation by addressing seven local churches. These churches were located in Asia Minor, modern Turkey. To five of these seven churches, the commander-in-chief underlined perseverance. To the church in Ephesus, He commended their *"patient endurance"* (Revelation 2:2). The church in Smyrna was encountering severe suffering and persecution. Jesus promised, *"If you remain faithful even when facing death, I will give you the crown of life"* (2:10). Pergamum was described as *"the city where Satan has his throne"* (2:13), but the Lord Jesus applauded the Christians there for their loyalty (2:13). To the church in Thyatira, He recognized their *"patient endurance"* (2:19). And to the Christians in Philadelphia, He promised, *"Because you have obeyed my command to persevere, I will protect you"* (3:10). These words are a reminder that you combat severe adversity with severe endurance. And we have received an exhortation from God to persevere to the end.

WE SHALL GO ON TO THE END

It is the same spirit demonstrated by Winston Churchill in the defining speech of World War II, delivered by him on June 4, 1940. German forces were in France and preparing to launch an invasion against England, which had the potential of bringing Great Britain to its knees. But the British would not go down without a fight. The heart of the nation—the hearts of the people—would not break. Churchill stood nose to nose with Hitler.

> Even though large parts of Europe and many old and famous States have fallen or may fall into the grip of the Gestapo and all the odious apparatus of Nazi rule, we shall not flag or fail. We shall go on to the end, we shall fight in France, we shall fight on the seas and oceans, we shall fight with growing confidence and growing strength in the air, we shall defend our Island, whatever the cost may be, we shall fight on the beaches, we shall fight on the landing grounds, we shall fight in the fields and in the streets, we shall fight in the hills; we shall never surrender.[3]

As the oration intensifies, you note that it is as though Churchill is preparing his people to fight a losing battle. They are first fighting on foreign soil. They lose that struggle and retreat to the seas and air, but with "growing" confidence and strength. Next, they withdraw to the defense of their own beaches. The retreat continues to the landing grounds. They find themselves in combat in the fields and in the very streets where their homes are located. Even there, they lose ground and withdraw to the hills. But despite the way things look, they are resolved not to give up the fight. They will never surrender. It was that resolve and spirit of perseverance that was, in my opinion, the turning point in the war.

Two weeks later, on June 18, 1940, Churchill delivered his "finest hour" speech. France had been overrun. Churchill spoke, "I expect that the Battle of Britain is about to begin … Let us therefore brace ourselves to our duties, and so bear ourselves, that if the British Empire and its Commonwealth last for a thousand years, men will still say, 'This was their finest hour.'"[4] That's *hupomonai*. Perseverance. Steadfast endurance.

Several years ago, Diane and I visited London, England. During our time in London, we visited Churchill's secret underground war rooms. The rooms had only recently opened up to the public, and one could view them just as they had been left many years before. A must see. The rooms were very small. In one of them, Churchill spent the night on a single bed. We were told he would wake up to the morning newspaper. If the news was good, he would immediately get up. If the news was bad, he would lie in bed for another half hour with the newspaper over his head. He felt the sting of defeat. But he would not let it prevail. He would then roll out of bed, call his cabinet together, and plan the next step. It was in one of these small rooms, around a small table, that Churchill's cabinet made decisions that would determine the outcome of the war.

I was most intrigued by something Churchill would not allow. He forbade any of his cabinet members to ever use the word *defeat* because triumph was the only option. And this was the spirit that resulted in *victory!* Don't ever give up too soon.

KEEPING ON KEEPING ON

My mother was a British nurse in London during those years of intense conflict. She endured the war, but, most notably, the summer and fall of 1940, when Hitler launched his most aggressive bombing campaign against Britain. The Battle of Britain. The German air force, Luftwaffe, blitzed the city of London every night, relentlessly, for six months. Every night as dusk fell, the sirens would sound. The small, gutsy British Spitfires would respond in the air, dipping and diving, as they confronted the heavy enemy planes coming in waves. My mother would leave work, throw on her tin hat, and run down the street heading for the Victoria Station just as the bombs were beginning to fall. Victoria Station sat in the shadow of Big Ben, chiming out the time and holding its post, vulnerable but defiant. She kept her ears attuned to the roar of any aircraft getting louder or the whistle of a bomb dropping. A searchlight scanning the sky overhead would catch a German bomber in its beam. Immediately, other searchlights would focus on the same aircraft. Once several searchlights had it in their crosshairs, all antiaircraft guns would unleash their fury on that one plane. What made the situation particularly hazardous was that the bomber would immediately unload its entire cargo of bombs. They would fall from the sky, hitting anyone, anything, anywhere.

Shelters were located at intervals along the stet. My mother would be quick to take shelter whenever she needed. The shelters would not withstand a direct hit, but gave protection from flying shrapnel. When she finally arrived at the train station, she would take the overland train home. There was never a guarantee of a way home, depending on what tracks had been blown out. When she finally arrived at her local station, her dad, my grandfather, would be there to meet her with his tin hat, and together they would run the final three-quarter mile home through gunfire and shrapnel. They didn't stop until they reached the shelter.

It was called an Anderson shelter. Her mother would greet her with a plate of food—rationed food—and a thermos of tea. She would spend the night with her family and a neighbouring family, six people, in the bomb shelter just large enough for a double-bed mattress. My grandfather had constructed the shelter in their backyard. It consisted of sheets of corrugated steel that had to be bolted together and buried in the ground. He had dug a hole four feet down and built the small dome-like structure inside the hole. The dirt that came out of the hole was used to cover the shelter, giving it the look of an earthen igloo and providing an additional valuable protection of two feet of dirt. A small tube was inserted through a tiny hole in the roof to allow for air. The air tube had a cap on the top to guard against shrapnel being blown down into the interior of the shelter.

The entrance was a small, heavy wooden door. Sometimes my mother would peek out through the door just to see what was happening. Everything was pitch black except for the light of explosions and searchlights. But her curiosity was soon overcome by the sense of danger. The sirens wailed. The ground shook as the big lorries drove up and down the streets hauling the massive antiaircraft guns. They would spend the long night hours listening to the whistling of the bombs and the explosions so frightfully close. The bombs seemed to fall in groups of five. The occupants of the small shelter frequently prayed, "Lord, protect us!" One night, a bomb hit very close. Then the next. And the next. And the next. With each crash the noise grew louder. My grandfather quietly said, "The next one is ours." They waited for number five to hit, but it didn't. Where was it? It just didn't come. Maybe it was a dud. God protected them many times. But it was absolute terror. One night, a bomb hit so close that the ceilings of their house came crashing down and all of the windows were blown out. My mother remembers the dining room buffet. It resembled a porcupine covered with four-inch shards of sharp glass protruding from its surface. She spent many days pulling out the long shards of glass. We have that buffet in our home as a reminder of those days.

When morning broke, the all-clear sirens would sound. They had survived another night. A new day had dawned. My mother would adorn herself in her shelter coat. This was a heavy, warm felt coat with a hood that her mother had made. It provided warmth and protection. It had big pockets where she could carry her identification cards, a flashlight, and bandages. It was dark red, enabling rescuers to find her more easily if she was ever buried in debris. She would then repeat the risk and routine all over again. This persisted for six long, endless months. They lived on rations and sheer guts. Life had to go on. Life must go on. And that is the spirit of perseverance and resolve we need to recapture when we hit walls in our lives. Walls are not the time to quit. They are the time to persevere. We must face severe trial with severe endurance.

PERSEVERING WITH JOY?

It is significant to note a short phrase the writer inserts in Hebrews 10:34. It is intentional and must not be missed. When these early Christians hit the wall of persecution, they *"accepted it with joy."* Now let's not confuse joy with happiness. Happiness is an emotion, a normal changing response to changing circumstances. When you go to a wedding, it is a time of happiness. When you attend a funeral, it is a time of sadness. Something would be odd if you didn't feel these emotions under these circumstances. But emotions are temperamental. Chameleonic—they change colour in accordance with the leaf you're sitting on. Mercurial—they rise or fall like the mercury in a thermometer, depending on the surrounding temperature.

Joy is different. Joy is a fruit of the Spirit. It goes much deeper. I used to do some scuba diving. At the surface of the lake, the air could be cold, the wind blustery, and the water turbulent. But fifty feet down all was peaceful and calm. A different world. Small fish swim right up to your mask to take a curious look at this strange visitor. Despite the turbulent circumstances in your life on the surface, to which the emotions respond, down deep in the core of your being is a strange calmness. An inner steadfast peace. Why? The Spirit of God is living His life down in there. Emotions are linked to life's variable circumstances around you. Fruit is linked to the One who is Life, living within you. When the Spirit of life and peace is within, the storm may blow against you, but you are anchored to Him. You know it. You feel it. That's joy in the storm.

Accepting something with joy doesn't mean that you have to pretend to be happy. It's not a "praise the Lord, anyway" kind of thing. We learned earlier that we need to be honest with our feelings. We need to be authentic with God. It is not a negative thing with God to feel the full brunt of pain in your life. You can cry out to God in your pain. But you can still experience joy.

The word *joy* points to two reasons for accepting your struggles and persevering in them. The first is recorded in Hebrews 10:34: *"You knew there were better things waiting for you that will last forever."* Then in verse 36, *"Then you will receive all that he has promised."* The first reason has to do with where you are going. If you know Jesus, you know that no matter how difficult the journey may be today, every step takes you closer to something better. Eternal joy. Eternal reward. The end of pain. Heaven. You will be home. If you truly know Jesus, you will do anything, endure anything, journey any distance—like Mary Draper Ingles or my mother—just to get where you most want to be. Home. You are familiar with the line, "Some people are so heavenly minded that they are no earthly good." I would respond that the Bible teaches the opposite. You are to be so heavenly minded that you are most earthly good. Hold fast to an eternal perspective. Keep your mind on heaven. Keep your head pointed home. Feel the warmth and joy of home. And keep going.

The second reason has to do with what you are becoming. James 1:2 states, *"When troubles come your way, consider it an opportunity for great joy."* There seems something oxymoronic here. Trouble, an opportunity for joy? Even great joy? Why? How can this be? It's because trouble is the soil of transformation. Note that James doesn't say *if* trouble comes, but *when* trouble comes. First, the wall of trial tests your faith (1:3). Severe trials force you to cling to God, the source of your strength. To place everything in His care and rest. To trust Him. To wait on Him, on His timing. It is the struggle that gives tenacity and grit to your faith. And then, as faith is tested, it grows endurance. Perseverance. And then, as endurance grows and develops, it grows character.

"You will be perfect and complete, needing nothing" (1:4). God's overarching, all-embracing will for your life is to be complete and perfect in character, Christ-like character. In other words, you are to be like Jesus, deep down inside. You have nothing to measure the depth of your character without the wall, and hitting the wall is the soil God cultivates to grow and deepen character. Struggle is an opportunity for growth, faith, endurance, character. In that order. The critical issue is not the resolving or removal of the trial, but the growth of Christ-like character through the trial. Hence, troubles are an opportunity for great joy because of what you are becoming. So persevere with joy. God is at work transforming your character into His likeness.

Ross' Story

I HAD SERVED THE COMPANY IN VARIOUS MANAGEMENT ROLES FOR thirty-one years. I had proven myself many times and was working on important initiatives. A couple of months ahead of time, the possibility of terminations had been leaked; 1,200 people would be let go from the company's 40,000 employees. This announcement was supposed to help everyone "get comfortable" with the concept. The vice president met with all the staff and clarified that, indeed, cutbacks were needed. He explained that if one's job were in question, one's manager would call.

It was just a short time later that my director poked her head into my office and asked if I would meet her in the small conference room. The walk to the small room felt more like a walk to an execution chamber. The conference room was a quiet, neutral room, empty except for a lone table and a few chairs that sat as silent witnesses to any proceedings. There was a Kleenex box in the centre of the table. The small box of tissues reinforced the milieu of doom. She explained how valuable I had been to the organization, but that my job was under review and it had been decided the company would be restructuring without me. I thought that I had prepared myself for the verdict, but the words left me frozen. She told me that I could stay for the rest of the month or leave today. I left that day.

Normal protocol of terminations provided for an immediate physical escort to the door. It was a most embarrassing experience.

Terminated. Escorted out. Jobless. Besieged with an overriding sense of disappointment and rejection. Walls.

Looking Sideways at the Wall

9

MARK AND I WERE TWO SEMINARIANS AND SOON TO BE BROTHERS-in-law. We were looking forward to the next summer with anticipation. It seemed like a long way off, but we knew it would be upon us sooner than later. Our vision was to share the gospel with the young men in the Junior Ranger Camps in Northern Ontario. These seventeen- and eighteen-year-old men were hired to spend the summer months in some of the most out-of-the-way areas in the north, planting trees, building roads, and fighting forest fires. They would work hard all day and return at day's end to enjoy a hearty supper. They would then spend the evenings with very little to do. Our plan was to drive into camp and ask permission to spend the evening interacting with the guys. We would play our guitars and show a film designed to generate discussion around the questions, "Is there a God?" and "Does it matter?"

We really believed this was what God wanted us to do for the summer. We planned for the venture all year. We shared our vision with churches all over Southern Ontario. There was surprising enthusiasm for what we were anticipating to do. People gave financially. They promised to pray. We collected tons of canned food. Mark's father donated an old half-ton truck that didn't look like it would make it over the next hill, let alone roll over the roads of Northern Ontario. But that's what God gave us, and we believed it would make the trip with gas in the tank, a wing, and a prayer. Well, lots of prayer. We painted it turquoise blue. (We thought that it looked good.) We built plywood sleeping quarters over the box, complete with a gate at the back for entry and, yes, mosquito-proof screening. We then filled the box with canned food and enough bug repellent to fend off every bug below the tree line. And off we went.

Our plans were to travel directly north to Sudbury. Then west along the north shore of Lake Huron to Sault Ste. Marie. We had grown up near the Soo and knew the area well. Then we planned to head north again to Wawa, home of the wild goose. We had mapped out the location of every Junior Ranger Camp along the north shore of Lake Superior. We even had a letter of permission from the Ontario minister of Natural Resources in Toronto, giving us access to the camps.

The first night went well. Better than we had ever anticipated. We showed our film and had a great discussion with the guys. We were so well received that we were invited to stay the night in the bunkhouse and leave the next morning after a breakfast of bacon, eggs, ham, potatoes, and pancakes. We were not to see food like that for the next eight weeks. That morning our old half-ton seemed to float on a cloud, its tires humming over the pavement, right into the next Ranger Camp.

STOP SIGN

The foreman met us at the gate. We could sense that he viewed us with suspicion. In fact, he flatly refused us permission. We produced our letter of permission, our lifesaver. He ran his eye over the print with a scowl and told us bluntly that he didn't want anything religious in his camp and that the only letter he would read would be one from the chief superintendent in Sudbury. That's when it hit us. We had grown up in the north. Nothing from the south carried any credibility. This was *Northern* Ontario. We could manage our own affairs and didn't need any interference from Southern Ontario. This welcome had been worse than we had anticipated. We put our tail between our legs and proceeded toward Sudbury, another hour up the highway. Old Blue didn't hum like before. She choked and grunted her way over the hills. She seemed to be in touch with our deflated emotions as her tires made their rotation with certain heaviness. Every bump was felt.

We reached Sudbury. We found the offices of the chief superintendent. We informed the secretary at the desk why we were there and asked for an appointment with her boss. She said he was busy. We expected that. She said he would see us at his earliest convenience. So we waited. And waited. And waited. At the end of the day, nothing. As the secretary was shutting off the office lights, she handed us a note. What we read was not a surprise by now. We had had all day to figure out the expected response. "Permission not granted." We hadn't even been granted a hearing. We left.

Now what? We had planned this whole venture. We believed God had led us to be here. We thought we had covered all the bases. We had expected challenges and obstacles, but we hadn't expected to hit this wall. How could we go back to the churches and friends who had supported us? How do you say, "We're back," two days after you've left? And what do we do with all this food and bug spray?

We were stuck in Sudbury. Mark knew a friend who lived in the city and called him. Yes, we could stay with him. We stayed that night. And the next. Praying. Processing what to do. How to return home and still save face?

DETOUR

It was early that second night when an answer came. God spoke.

"You've hit a wall?"

"Yes!"

"Your plans have fallen through?"

"Yes!"

"Have you considered that maybe your plans are not My plans? That this wall you've hit is from Me?"

"No! Really?"

"Yes. Look sideways from the wall. You'll see another direction. Go there."

"Go where?"

"Go north, straight north. I'll be waiting for you."

It suddenly made sense. The whole region north of Sudbury and west to Chapleau was outside the jurisdiction of the chief superintendent in Sudbury. We had been so intent on following our plans—or how to make the best retreat—that we had failed to consider that the Holy Spirit might be saying something else. We fell into bed that night ready to say goodbye to Sudbury—and our plans—and to wake up to a new day.

Old Blue started with the first turn of the key. She was purring again. Her tires hummed over the asphalt. We reflected on what we had learned already. Walls have a purpose. Wisdom says to look sideways from the wall to discern whether or not God might be opening up a new direction. We learned that this venture, just like the venture of life, needed to be supported by a lot of prayer.

That summer was a wonderful success. Old Blue took us down stretches of gravel road that seemed neverending. She got us through marsh and muskeg into bush camps hidden deep in the jack pine forests. Some nights we slept in the bush camps. Most nights, we slept in a gravel pit or on the edge of a river or lake. Before going to bed, we would spray the sleeping quarters with a generous amount of bug spray from our stock. Then we would slam the tailgate shut and run like crazy men around the pit or through the trees. This was a maneuver designed to outrun and outwit any mosquitoes that might be thinking about spending the night in our makeshift cabin. Arriving back at the truck, we would jump into the back as fast as possible before any mosquitoes realized what was happening. We kept a mosquito coil burning for the sake of the sand flies—we called them "no-see-ums"—that were small enough to fly right through the screen and turn your night into living torment.

Each evening in the camps was different. We would drive all day not knowing what our reception would be. Sometimes we were welcomed as though they were expecting us and waiting for us to arrive. A few times we were told to turn around and not come back. At some camps we talked long into the night in the bunkhouse, sharing our faith and answering questions from the Bible. We left Bibles in the hands of those who asked for one. On a few occasions we aroused anger and hostility. One could strongly sense the presence of the evil one trying to interfere and disrupt. But that summer we shared our faith. The seed of the good news about Jesus was sown in many hearts. Several young men gave their lives to Jesus.

A CHANGED PATH

Personally, I have learned that when you hit a wall in your life, one of the things to consider is whether God might be pointing you in a new direction. The New Testament word for *revelation* means "to uncover, to unveil, to reveal something that is hidden." Walls often lead to a revelation.

Recently, I read an article about Michael J. Fox. Michael was born in Burnaby, British Columbia. Most of us got to know Michael as Alex Keaton on the popular TV show *Family Ties*. The show won him three Emmys and one Golden Globe. He was a successful actor, riding the crest of the wave, at the top of his career. Then he hit the wall. Parkinson's disease. His life was derailed. Parkinson's is a chronic, degenerative neurological disorder that affects one in one hundred people over sixty years old. Michael was only thirty.

He tried to cover it up. He went on to star in *Spin City*, another successful show that won him one Emmy and three Golden Globes. After four years on *Spin City*, however, he could hide his condition no longer. He retired from the show and full-time acting. The wall of PD stopped him from proceeding in the direction in which he had been going. But it did not stop him. About the same time he founded the Michael J. Fox Foundation and dedicated himself to finding a cure for Parkinson's Disease.

> "There are things that I can't do to the extent that I used to do or, in some cases, at all," admits Fox. "But there are more things that I do that I didn't do before. We sometimes see subtractions when we're ill. They're not just subtractions. I'm not me minus anything; I'm me plus this experience. Whether it's good or bad is a subjective thing, but this has assuredly changed my path. And changed the way I look at things. Changed the things I do. I started this foundation; I wrote two books now. I've had experiences meeting people and travelling I never would have had. I've seen the reaction people have to my message, which is a positive message and a message [that] we can change things not out of panic but out of hope and a sense of purpose."[1]

Fox has written a book titled *Always Looking Up: The Adventures of an Incurable Optimist*. It is significant that he does not say incurable disease, but incurable optimist. He writes, "For everything this disease has taken, something of greater value has been given—sometimes just a marker that points me in a new direction that I might not otherwise have traveled."[2]

Walls do that. They often point you in a direction you might not otherwise have travelled. They change the way you look at things. They change your life. Can you imagine the potential for a life when it is the providential hand of God that is operative, using the wall to reveal something new? To open up an alternative? To reveal a fresh opportunity? To unveil new meaning for your life?

THE CONVERSION THAT CHANGED THE WORLD

Talk about a new direction. There was a man in the Bible who hit the wall and experienced a titanic change in his life. Everything changed. His name was Saul. It was a time in the history of the church when there was great hostility and persecution directed toward it. And Saul was at the eye of the storm. He was the instigator, a fanatical persecutor of the young fledgling church, harassing and oppressing anyone who followed the Way of Jesus. The Scriptures put it this way: *"A great wave of persecution began that day, sweeping over the church… … Saul was going everywhere to destroy the church. He went from house to house, dragging out both men and women to throw them into prison"* (Acts 8:1–3). Saul was radically defending his own faith. He honestly believed Jesus was a messianic imposter and that His followers, who were spreading this new faith about Him, should be eliminated. *"Saul was uttering threats with every breath and was* eager *to kill the Lord's followers"* (Acts 9:1, emphasis added). This man was a passionate Christ-hater and a despiser of anyone who professed the name of Jesus.

And then Saul hit the wall. He was on his way to Damascus to find and arrest any followers of "the Way" (9:2). That's when he ran into Jesus. It was like hitting a train. His horse bolted, and Saul fell to the ground blinded by a light brighter than the sun. It was unexpected and dramatic. Saul later gave a firsthand account of what happened that day when everything changed. *"About noon … as I was on the road, a light from heaven brighter than the sun shone down on me and my companions. We all fell down, and I heard a voice saying to me in Aramaic, 'Saul, Saul, why are you persecuting me? It is useless for you to fight against my will'"* (Acts 26:13–14). Saul, blind and fumbling around on the dirt road, was picked up and led by the hand. Humbled and helpless. He had hit a wall, and he would never be the same again. Neither would the world.

This was what I call a wall revelation. The unveiling of the One whom Saul was persecuting. The stripping of Saul's pride and arrogance. The uncovering of a new life. The revelation of a new direction. The great persecutor of the good news about Jesus was to become the great proclaimer of the good news about Jesus. Jesus unveiled Saul's new path and purpose. Saul set out earlier that day *"armed with the authority and commission of the leading priests"* (Acts 26:12) and ended the day armed with the authority and commission of Jesus Christ.

> *Get to your feet! For I have appeared to you to appoint you as my servant and witness. You are to tell the world what you have seen and what I will show you in the future … Yes, I am sending you to the Gentiles to open their eyes, so they may turn from darkness to light and from the power of Satan to God. Then they will receive forgiveness for their sins and be given a place among God's people, who are set apart by faith in me* (Acts 26:16–18).

NEW MEANING

When Saul hit the wall that day, it was a time of unveiling new meaning for his life. Saul, who was later called Paul, could have had nightmares about the awful pain he had inflicted upon so many people whose only crime was that they loved and followed Jesus. Rather, he chose not to play the old tapes, but to play a new tape. *"[Christ] considered me trustworthy and appointed me to serve him, even though I used to blaspheme the name of Christ"* (1 Timothy 1:12–13). He recognized that he had been appointed by Jesus to serve Him.

Paul added,

> *Christ Jesus came into the world to save sinners—and I am the worst of them all. But God had mercy on me so that Christ Jesus could use me as a prime example of his great patience with even the worst sinners. Then others will realize that they, too, can believe in him and receive eternal life* (1 Timothy 1:15–16).

The new meaning in Paul's life embraced the reality that he was exhibit A for the power and patience of God to save and transform a human life, and that if He could do it for Paul, He can do it for anybody.

THE UNEXPECTED

When you hit the wall, you may discover something you didn't expect. There is a well-known story in Genesis 22. It is the account of Abraham when God told him to take his only son, Isaac, his son of promise, his son whom he loved with everything in him, to a mountain to sacrifice him to the Lord. This must have ripped the heart out of Abraham. This was an unprecedented wall for Abraham. I am a father and grandfather. I can't imagine it. While God's command may sound pretty archaic and repulsive to us living in the twenty-first century, God was testing Abraham's faith and obedience. Human sacrifice was common in the religions and culture of Abraham's day. But it was not God's intention that Abraham would offer his son as a human sacrifice. This was repulsive to God Himself. Just as Abraham lifted the knife, God stopped him.

At that point, Abraham looked around and sighted a ram caught by its horns in a thicket. He quickly untied his son and took the ram and sacrificed it to the Lord in the place of his son. The Lord had wonderfully provided. Abraham was so moved that he named the place Yahweh-Yireh, which means "the Lord will provide." Over time, this became a proverb repeated by people over and over again: "On the mountain of the Lord it will be provided." It is equally true that when you hit the wall in your life, the Lord will provide. And one of the ways He provides is by redirecting you to look sideways and discover something new, often unexpected.

MAYDAY!

While growing up as a young boy, I was made familiar with the concept of looking sideways at the wall. I never thought of it in those terms, but I was made cognizant of its reality. As I already mentioned, my parents experienced firsthand the tumultuous years of World War II. My mother was a British nurse in London, England. And my father was a Canadian soldier. There were stories they told us as children, although there was much that, even to this day, they would not or could not talk about. But there were stories that entrenched themselves into my mind. One of those stories taught me at an early age that sometimes God uses the wall to accentuate His way in one's life. It is like an exclamation mark; it gets your attention. It turns your head in a new direction. It sensitizes your hearing to the voice of God. It clarifies calling.

My father was only twenty years old. He was with a regiment called the Canadian Grenadier Guards. He rode as the wireless operator in a thirty-five-ton Sherman tank. They were involved in a pincer movement in the hills of northwest Holland near the German border, near the small town of Gronigen. There were three squadrons of tanks, fifteen tanks in all, and an infantry unit following along behind the line of tanks. About one hundred and seventy-five men in all.

They found a suitable place to stop for the night. There was a barn nearby. The tanks positioned themselves around the barn, camouflaged behind small grassy hillocks, their big guns, barely visible, pointed out over the mounds. The infantry set up about one hundred and fifty machine guns ready to go if needed. Those men who were not on guard duty were permitted to enjoy a much-needed sleep inside the shelter of the barn. Normally, nights were spent in a coffin-like hole under the tank. A trench was dug and then the tank was driven over the trench to provide cover. The men would crawl under the tank to sleep. It was often cold and damp. This night would be different. Most men pulled themselves up onto the hayloft and stretched themselves out for a good night's sleep. Three or four soldiers, including my father, were a little more cautious and opted to crawl under a hay wagon to sleep.

About midnight, there was a terrific explosion. German soldiers had somehow crept through gaps in the lines and around the guards and thrown a sticky bomb up onto the roof of the barn. The whole roof blew up and came crashing in upon the sleeping men. Many were killed and many others wounded. The sky lit up as tracer bullets saturated the blackness of the night. Flares illuminated the surrounding fields, exposing the infiltrators. For a time it seemed like hell really had erupted. Chaos. Confusion. The clamour of panicking men. The noise of one hundred and fifty machine guns unleashing their fury all at once. Something had hit my father, giving him a deep inch-and-a-half-long wound on the side of the head. He could feel a trickle of blood running down over his cheek. It was at that moment my father hit a wall. He thought this was an ordeal which he would not survive. He cried out to God. "O God, help me! If You will get me out of this alive, I will do whatever You want for the rest of my life."

"Mayday" is an international signal indicating that a ship or an aircraft is in distress. "We're hit! We're going down!" It is a call for immediate help. It comes from the French *m'aidez* meaning "help me!" It is the kind of call people cry out when they fear for their lives. Well, this was the prayer on the lips of my father that night. "Mayday! Help me!" And God heard it.

An officer charged into the barn and yelled, "All able-bodied men, OUT!" My father responded, "Sir, I think that I've been shot!" The commanding officer retorted, "If you're on your feet, you're okay. OUT!" My father answered with an immediate leap through an opening in the wall. Under the light from the flares, he bounded toward the safety of his tank.

MAYDAY TWO!

But that is only part one of a three-part story. The date was May 8, 1945. The last day of the war. The whole horrendous thing had finally officially ended, one day before my father's twenty-first birthday. The place was northwest Germany. German soldiers were pouring in from the towns and fields, surrendering themselves and their weapons. My father was on guard duty, perched atop the turret of the tank. The heavy Sherman tank was parked in a swamp, its large gun peeking out through the bulrushes.

My father was frustrated and fearful. Frustrated, because he could not hear well. The bulrushes were rustling loudly as a persistent wind blew through them. Fearful, because he felt like a sitting target for a sniper. He thought to himself, "Great. I survive this war, and then get killed the last night, the night before my twenty-first birthday." His fears were well founded. Among the thousands of men surrendering their weapons, there were some fanatics intent on taking a final shot and taking someone out.

Four days after the war had ended, tragedy struck within my father's own Regiment. A new young chaplain had recently arrived on the front with the Regiment. A fresh graduate from Toronto Bible College. His name was Captain McCreery. Young McCreery made a strong, positive impression on the men. He introduced himself to them: "I am honoured to be your padre but I would prefer to be one of your troop leaders."[3]

Less than a month later, he was accompanying another officer, Lieutenant Goldie, on a mercy mission in a Jeep, picking up wounded German soldiers off the battlefield. Neither returned. A patrol was sent out to find them, but there was no trace. Two days later, McCreery's body was discovered. A sniper's bullet had found him first.[4] He is on record as the last Canadian soldier to be killed in the war. This was my father's padre. It was during these final days of the war when my father felt the obsessive shadowy presence of the wall, and he cried out to God again, "God, if You'll get me out alive, I'll do whatever You want for the rest of my life." "Mayday! Help!" A desperate call. And God heard it.

MAYDAY THREE!

As I said, there are three parts to the story. Fast-forward twenty years. My father married my mother. They returned to Canada. He found a job with the T. Eaton Company and advanced from serving in the coffee bar to becoming the assistant manager of one of the Eaton stores. All this time God had been calling him to full-time ministry as a pastor. Now, we should all be in full-time ministry for Christ, and my parents were busily engaged in serving God in numerous ways. But in my dad's case, God had been calling him to be a pastor. Things had been going well in business. In fact, my father had just received an invitation to become the manager of the T. Eaton store in Sault Ste. Marie, Ontario.

It was at this time that he hit the wall again. He became very ill. He was increasingly losing strength and would often come home midday from work only to rest. The doctors examined and reexamined him all to no avail. My mother gathered all four children around her one day and explained to us that there was a strong possibility that we would be losing our dad. She was preparing us for the worst. We prayed as a family. It was another Mayday prayer. "God, we are desperate. Please help us, now! Mayday!"

Then it happened. One night, God rewound my father back twenty years. He took him back to those two occasions in the war when he really felt up against the wall. Times when he surrendered himself to whatever God wanted for his life. Times when God instilled in him a sense of direction. Times when he looked sideways from the wall and God revealed an unexpected path of service for him to take. He knew God had called him to be a pastor. Since that time he had taken a different path. But now it was as though God was giving him another chance. An opportunity to renew his vow to God. He'd hit another wall. A wall to stop him in his tracks. A wall from which to look sideways and rediscover and reclaim the path God had unveiled for his life. That night, Dad responded to the Lord, "Yes, Lord, I'll surrender."

The next morning, he woke my mother. He seemed to have a renewed strength. He recounted to her what had happened in the night. The Lord had spoken to him and reminded him of those times twenty years earlier when, against the wall, he had made some promises to God and God had unveiled His will to him. God was clearly saying to him, "Are you going to do what I want, or shall I take you home?"

That day, my father went to work and handed in his notice. People thought he had gone out of his mind. Why would he leave a successful career? Why walk away from a wonderful future opportunity? But he had been to the wall. God had clearly uncovered the path set for him. And he would follow. By the way, the next visit to the specialist uncovered the problem. It was as though God had removed the blinders from the eyes of the medical doctors. My father recovered.

The next time you hit the wall, look sideways. God may be revealing a new direction. Opening a new path. Unveiling new meaning for your life. Follow it.

MUSICAL CHAIRS

I should make it clear that not every wall is a painful or distressing experience. Pain is the most effective stimulus. But sometimes it can be just an annoyance. An aggravation. Just a normal set of circumstances that alters your course. It can be something innocuous, but which God uses to get you out of your seat and move you. Perhaps we need to be less resistant to these daily obstructions and move with them. Let me give you an illustration of what I mean.

Recently, Diane and I were returning from Peru. We were waiting at the airport in Lima. The waiting area at the gate was quickly filling with people, so we snatched one of the few vacant seats and sat down. I got up for just a moment to speak with someone across the aisle. When I turned around to return to my seat, someone else was sitting in it. I felt a little annoyed but had no choice but to look somewhere else. There were only a few available seats, so I quickly found one and claimed it. I had barely planted myself when a rather large, grumpy man appeared out of nowhere and claimed the seat as his own. "You're sitting in my seat," he snapped. My annoyance level went up a few degrees. I couldn't see his name on the seat. And I wasn't sitting on his luggage. But neither did I want to start a seat war. So I calmly got up, said that I was sorry, and went in search of another place to park my derriere.

There was only one seat available by this point. It was beside a young man. He was rather scruffy looking with an old straw hat pulled down over his disheveled hair. His backpack was between his knees. I sat down beside him. I don't think he even noticed me sit down. He was intently writing in a journal. I honestly tried not to peek, but my curiosity got the better of me, and I leaned a little closer without appearing to do so. That could have been embarrassing. He seemed to be writing in an angry sort of way. He was writing about the people sitting around him. Well, that was now me. So I kept my eye to the notepad. He described them as arrogant, insensitive, loud, self-centred. Something in me wanted desperately to inform him that I was a Canadian and was not loud or arrogant unless at a hockey game. But another voice within gently urged me to open up a conversation with him just out of interest in him.

I ventured a question. "So what brings you to Peru?" He seemed rather surprised that anyone would open up a conversation, but he answered that he was a university student from the U.S. who had come to Lima for six weeks to strengthen his language skills in Spanish. I told him I was a Canadian (I felt a load lift) and that we were here to visit churches and orphanages in the mountains just outside Lima. I told him I was coming away very impressed with the work that was being done with so many needy children. He seemed curious and asked me what I meant. I told him I witnessed so many Christian workers doing so much to assist and bring hope to the lives of children and families out of pure love for people and Jesus.

I told him my name and asked him for his. It was John. He offered some information. He responded that he had read a few religious books but hadn't found what he was looking for. I asked him what he was looking for. And the conversation just opened up as an opportunity for me to share with him the difference between religion and Christ. I shared my faith in Jesus with him, and he listened intently. When I touched on the resurrection of Jesus, he stopped me and asked if I really believed that. I told him why I did. The time for boarding was just minutes away. The hour had swept by. I asked him if he owned a Bible. He didn't. I kicked myself that I didn't have mine; I would have given it to him. It was packed and checked in. But he promised me he would get a Bible and read it. "Where should I start?" he asked. I suggested the four Gospels. He hadn't heard about them, nor did he know where to find them in a Bible. I explained. He wrote everything down in his notepad. His seat was called, and he was off. We waved goodbye. But I don't think that was the end of John's story. It was clear to me that this was a divine appointment. God had blocked my path twice just to direct me to him.

The next time God plays musical chairs with you, don't get annoyed. Play along. Understand that God might be redirecting you to look sideways. He might be uncovering a fresh opportunity. Watch for where God is taking you.

Bonnie's Story

I RAN SMACK UP AGAINST MY WALL WHEN I WAS ASKED BY MY HUSBAND'S urologist to come with him to someplace private so that he could give me the results of what we thought was a simple prostate procedure. Eventually, the dreaded C word was used. Barry's bladder was full of cancer. So it wasn't a small prostate problem; it was a big cancer problem.

That evening I wrote in my journal: "All I can remember about today is that suddenly without warning my world has come crashing down around me, and I feel all alone and oh so scared." It was decided Barry should have chemotherapy before surgery with the hope of shrinking the growth. Twelve sessions of chemotherapy later, I wrote in my journal: "Hopes were dashed today as the latest CAT scan shows that the chemotherapy has done absolutely nothing. So another one of those very low points in this, our faith journey. Lord, I want to be gracious and accepting, but why? Why Barry? Why this? Why didn't the chemo work? Fear has replaced the calm, and I struggle to be strong. How are we going to tell our family and friends? I feel liked I'm in a dark tunnel and can't even see a light at the end of it."

Barry had his surgery, and the bladder was removed. We felt a sense of hope again. One year later, however, the cancer returned. This time in Barry's right lung. More surgery. More chemo. Six months later, cancer was found in his left lung. More surgery. Then cancer was discovered in his right lung again. More surgery. Friends and family tried to strengthen us. Prayer was offered up all over the world. But the wall seemed to be growing higher, overshadowing everything. We kept climbing. Persevering.

I will never forget that disheartening conversation in the oncologist's office. "Barry, you have stage 4 cancer." Stage 4 cancer! I asked what that meant. I soon learned. There was no stage 5 cancer. I now understood that unless God intervened, I was going to lose my earthly best friend, my biggest ally, my protector, provider, counsellor, and lover to this nasty disease called cancer.

The wall seemed insurmountable. I was scared. How would I cope alone? My mind began to congest with disturbing thoughts. Financial security. Wills. Power of attorney. Funeral arrangements. Fear consumed me. Then anxiety. Then depression. I wasn't sure if I could talk with Barry about the things on my mind—I didn't want to upset him. Satan began to taunt me, "Where's your faith now?" I had always been an organized person. But at this point things were piling up at home and work, and I didn't know where to begin. It became difficult to make decisions. I finally went to see a Christian counsellor. I was told that what I was experiencing had a name—anticipatory grief. It was normal. WOW! I was normal.

God came to me at my wall in so many ways. A verse of Scripture. A word of inspiration that sprang out at me from my inbox. A feeling of deep peace that settled over me. An act of kindness. A hug. A card. A song. A multitude of reminders that as I walked through this valley of shadows, He really was with me. And He would provide for me. And He did promise to hold tomorrow and me in His hands.

10 God Meets You at the Wall

I LOVE THE SMELL OF AN OLD BOOK. I AM HOLDING AN OLD BOOK IN my hands called *Night Scenes in the Bible* by Daniel March. It is dated 1869. Its cover is thick leather, and engraved into its aged leather skin in gold letters are the title and the words, "God spoke to Israel in visions of the night." The pages are yellowed and worn. Dispersed throughout its pages are beautiful and detailed ink etchings of night scenes from the Bible. In this book, March walks into the lives and experiences of people who encountered God during the night hours. For me, the book is really a memory aid, reminding me that God often comes to us and speaks during the dark hours of life.

Daniel March addressed two chapters to the old patriarch, Jacob. The first chapter is titled, "Jacob's Night at Bethel." Jacob was running from home, from the wrath of his brother Esau. His deceitful nature had finally caught up with him, and he was on the run. He would never see his parents again. Jacob's problem, however, was one that we all have. He could not run from himself. I take me wherever I go. So do you. We can run from our problems, but not from ourselves.

Jacob had hit the wall. That was when God came to him in a vision. A ladder appeared, stretching from heaven to earth, from God right down to where Jacob lay. God then spoke to him, giving him a promise. *"I am with you, and I will protect you wherever you go. One day I will bring you back to this land. I will not leave you"* (Genesis 28:15). Jacob's response? *"Surely the Lord is in this place, and I wasn't even aware of it!*" (28:16). This is too often the truth. God comes to you during the dark night of your soul. And if you are not sensitive to His presence or listening for His voice, you completely miss Him. He is in this space with you, and you are unaware of Him. How tragic.

The second chapter about Jacob is called "Jacob's Night of Wrestling." Yes, that was another dark night. This time he was returning home after years of exile. Many things had changed. He was married, had a family, and possessed more wealth than he knew what to do with. But some things hadn't changed. Or so it would seem. Jacob was barely into familiar surroundings, travelling down the Jabbok River, when he got the news that his brother Esau, who was the excuse for fleeing in the first place, was coming to meet him with four hundred armed men. Well, it didn't take a brain to know that this didn't look good. And this time, it wasn't just himself that Jacob had to worry about. He had a family that he must care for. Jacob hit the wall again.

That night, under cover of darkness, Jacob sent his family and everything he owned across the ford of the Jabbok. Then he retreated back across the Jabbok to spend the night alone.

I still remember the day I made my way up the Jabbok in a Jeep. The Jabbok flows out into the Jordan River from the east side. My brother and I were searching for Penuel, an archaeological site in Jordan and the site the Bible identifies as the place where our story occurred. It is a rugged land, and desolate, except for a few Bedouin leading their herds of sheep and goats and washing their clothes in the small flowing river. We came to a thin sign nailed to a post with the name *Penuel* written on it. There, rising up from the stony road, was the ancient tel. We climbed to the top to get a view of the topography and the river as it threaded its way through the craggy terrain.

At the base of Penuel was a ford, just as the Bible recorded. For centuries, the Bedouin have used it to cross with their herds. We spoke to an elderly Bedouin man who confirmed its use by the people of the region for ages. We took off our boots and crossed the shallow waters of the ford just the way Jacob had centuries before. On the east side of the ford was a small clearing. With a little imagination, I could picture what had happened one night centuries earlier. Not only was Esau coming to meet up with Jacob, but that night God had an appointment with Jacob. As Jacob was slipping into his sleeping bag, from out of the darkness appeared a shadowy figure. A divine wrestler. He leaped at Jacob and thus began a night of struggle. Back and forth. Neither giving up. Neither surrendering. Neither letting go. That is, until daybreak. At the first sign of dawn, the divine *wrestler* touched Jacob's hip. That's all it took. A touch. As Jacob began to fall, he tenaciously held on to his assailant. His eyes opened. He knew his assailant. He recognized the divine presence. He pressed for a blessing. He surrendered.

At that moment, Jacob knew he had been in God's presence. In fact, it was Jacob who gave this place its name. *Peniel* means "face of God." He had seen God face to face. As the sun rose that morning, Jacob walked with a limp because of the injury to his hip. When God comes to you in one of those dark times and touches your life, you will never be the same. You may walk with a limp from that time forward. But let that limp be a reminder to you not of failure, but of the time when God intervened in your life. And won.

CHAPTER 19 IN LIFE

And then there was Elijah. The champion of Carmel. The showdown at O.K. Carmel. Elijah faced down 850 pagan prophets and encountered fire from heaven and rain from the sky. You can read the story in 1 Kings 18. It was the high point in Elijah's life. Then comes chapter 19. Everything changed. Queen Jezebel threatened to hunt Elijah down and have him executed. And the champion, who had stood up to the powerful King Ahab and his throng of prophets, crumpled under the weight of Jezebel's threat. He fled for his life southward into the Negev desert, and got as far away as he could get. He travelled alone all day, and as evening approached, found a solitary tree and sat under it. Fear and a crushing sense of aloneness settled down upon him. It was here that he cried out in desperation, "Lord, I have had enough. Take my life. Let me die!"

Have you ever been there?

VULNERABILITY WHERE YOU LEAST EXPECT IT

It is noteworthy that this crushing period came after a time of success. A time of achievement. It was as though Elijah had reached the summit, raised the flag of Jehovah God, stepped back, and fallen off the pinnacle. The truth is you're never closer to defeat than at the moment of triumph. Never nearer failure than at a time of success. Never more vulnerable to discouragement than after a time of achievement and applause. There is a principle here too often overlooked. We are vulnerable in the area of our strengths. We are readily aware of our weaknesses and quick to fortify and strengthen those areas. We cry out to God in faith when in a time of known need. But how often do we stop to think that maybe the biggest temptation to a fall comes during the times of success and achievement? We become careless when things are going well. We don't think of the need to fortify our strengths.

There is a great illustration of this in Canadian history, a neglect in the area of strength that changed the course of history in North America. The year was 1759. The French and Indian War was well underway. The struggle was between the French with their Indian allies against the British over the control of North America. The French stronghold to the north was the walled fortress of Quebec. General James Wolfe, commander of the British troops, had laid siege to Quebec, but was unable to penetrate the solid defenses of the French. The prolonged siege was almost into its seventh month. It had been a period of frustration and failure. Wolfe had lost close to one thousand men—dead, wounded, or missing. The consensus of Wolfe's officers was to lift the siege, go home, and return at a later time. Wolfe refused to pull back. A plan was hatched. One last gamble.

Under cover of darkness, Wolfe floated his fleet up the St. Lawrence River, past the sleeping fortress, and anchored just one mile upstream from the city at the base of the steeply rising bluffs. The French did not expect an attack would ever come from this side of the city. The vertical cliffs which rose from the river were a natural strength and defense. What happened next was even more astonishing. Wolfe commanded his force of 4,800 men to scale the almost perpendicular heights. Wolfe's men began to silently climb the bluffs, grasping rocks, roots, or whatever they could clutch, dragging their heavy artillery with them piece by piece. By daybreak they had accomplished an incredible feat. The entire British force had scaled the heights up onto the plateau above. The plateau was known as the Plains of Abraham—named after the owner of the land, river pilot Abraham Martin. The plateau overlooked the fortress of Quebec.

The unsuspecting French defenders woke up that morning to columns of redcoats, guns poised and ready, lined up on the Plains of Abraham, atop the cliffs and peering down upon the fortress. The French general, Montcalm, rode his horse toward the Plains expecting to see a detachment of several hundred British soldiers. He was shocked to discover almost the entire British force. The Battle of Quebec had been determined. The French were defeated, and British dominance of North America began. The war was not over, but a fatal wound had been dealt.

It should never have happened that way. So why did it? The French defenders failed to watch and fortify their point of strength. They were careless about defense of the bluffs, because, well, no one would or could scale the heights, could they? The French failed to recognize their true vulnerability in the place where they least expected it. Maybe Elijah was experiencing something like this. Can we? Absolutely.

What wall did Elijah hit? It was a solid wall of fear. *"He was afraid and fled for his life"* (1 Kings 19:3). Afraid of man and circumstances. And, yes, they can do us harm. They can be threatening. They do give us reason to fear.

Elijah's wall was also a debilitating barricade of depression. Severe depression. *"'I have had enough, LORD," he said. 'Take my life, for I am no better than my ancestors who have already died'"* (1 Kings 19:4). Exhaustion. A sense of failure. It's a recipe for depression. Depression is a horrible wall. A crushing wall. A wall too often dismissed by others who do not understand it. You feel no energy or interest in anything. Lethargy and fatigue settle in. You feel useless, joyless, hopeless. Not only is there no light visible at the end of the tunnel, there is no visible end to the tunnel. It just seems to be cloudy and raining all of the time. As with Elijah, there are sometimes thoughts of death, even suicide.

God came to him. God understood his human frailty. He instructed him to get some sleep and some good nutritious food into his stomach. There is a physical component to recovery. Sleep. Nutrition. Medical attention. Personal attention. But understand that God knows your need and does not dismiss you.

Elijah travelled another forty days south into the desert. He arrived at Mount Sinai. There he discovered a cave and slipped into it for shelter for the night. God had followed him there and, of course, was there with him all the time. Now God came to him again and asked him what was going on. Elijah's response alerts us as to what the mortar was in the wall he had hit since Carmel. Aloneness. He spoke up that he had served God zealously. And yet he saw no fruit. No positive change in the people to whom he went. In fact, resistance and hostility abounded. He felt disappointed. Defeated. Useless. Vulnerable. Alone. He felt like he was the only one left.

Self-awareness is a good thing. It is healthy to come face to face with yourself. To know your frailty, your need, who you are—or aren't. That is until it is out of balance. By that, I mean you become more aware of who you are than of who God is in your life. True healthy balance is knowing who you are, and who God is.

LISTENING FOR GOD'S VOICE

God needed to give Elijah a spiritual alignment. So He met Elijah at the wall in chapter 19. It's usually chapter 19 in your life where you encounter God in unexpected ways. A tornado hit the mountain where Elijah waited, ripping the rocks from their place. But God was not in the tornado. Then, an earthquake rattled the mountain from its foundations. But God was not in the earthquake. Next, a fire blazed past Elijah. But God did not speak from the midst of the fire. You would expect to find God in the seismic things of life. And sometimes God does assault us like an armed assailant from behind the bush under the cover of darkness. Remember Jacob at the Jabbok? But not necessarily so.

After all the commotion of the seismic events, Elijah heard a gentle whisper. So quiet it would have gone unnoticed if he had not been listening. I wonder how many times God passes by, and we do not see

Him because we have our attention on so many other things. Our minds and spirits are focused on the wall before us rather than the One who comes to meet with us at the wall. I wonder how many times God speaks to us, and we do not recognize His voice because we are listening to too many other voices. Sometimes the voice of our pain cries so loudly that we wait for a louder voice, something seismic in proportion, to get our attention.

Do not miss the gentle whisper. Do not let that still voice of quiet affirmation escape you. That unassuming whisper of assurance. That consoling voice of hope. God's voice. The Spirit's nudge. It's holy ground. It's easy to miss. Earlier I noted that, when Jacob was running away from home and family, God came to him. Jacob admitted to being in God's presence and not knowing. When you arrive at chapter 19 in your own life, stay alert. Listen carefully.

God reminded Elijah that he might want to die, but that his life was not over until God's purpose for his life was over. There were two kings and one prophet to be anointed by Elijah as God's representative. There was still work to be done. It's good to remember that. God has a purpose for your life, and your life is not over until God's purpose for your life is over.

Then God gave Elijah a new perspective. God would preserve Elijah's life and provide for him, but there were more than Elijah to care for. Sometimes your pain and loneliness can become so great that that's all you see and feel. Yes, there were more. Many more. Seven thousand others in Israel who had never worshipped Baal or surrendered to the pressures of the pagan culture. Elijah was not alone. He just felt that way. A healthy perspective when you hit chapter 19. When you hit the wall and your pain closes in on you, remember you're not alone. There are others. God cares for them. And He cares for you.

THE WALL

It doesn't seem that long ago when I hit the second major wall in my life. Being a pastor means there are times when you experience what could be termed pure joy. When you have a part in seeing someone give his or her life to Jesus, or when you witness transformation in a life, or a broken life restored, you feel pure joy. To open your Bible and teach the Scriptures is pure joy. Just to be where God wants you is pure joy. But there are other times when discouragement and even despair break in upon you, robbing you of any joy, and you feel the full weight of the church upon you. The scales are tipped by the gravity of pain. This was that kind of time.

There had been a spirit of unsettling resistance in the church for a long time by a few but influential people. The situation came to a head when the leadership had to release the chairman of our elders' board because of a breach of trust. That was a really difficult time. The attack upon me as a leader became increasingly intense and personal. I struggled with betrayal. There was a growing spirit of blame, misrepresentation, slander, broken confidentialities, and a nagging undercurrent of dissention.

It grew so severe that, for my own emotional health (I had lost twenty-five pounds in a few months) I temporarily stepped back from full-time ministry. God mercifully opened up two escapes for me. I continued on at the church as the teaching pastor but took on a part-time twelve-month contractual administrative position with a Bible college and seminary.

OUR BETHESDA

In addition, God led us to a new home outside of town in the country. It was a new home but not a new house. A work in progress and an adventure for our family. We gutted the house. We overhauled and underpinned. Remodeled, reconstructed, refashioned, renovated, and refinished. A lot of "re's," but it was a house in need of renewal, just like us. We did most of the work ourselves, with the help of friends, working through the evening until around 2:00 AM each day. Every night, each family member sought out a place to sleep, wherever there was the least amount of dust and construction. Through the winter months, we usually curled up in front of the lone wood-burning stove, our only source of heat, to keep warm. The mornings were a challenge. We had one functioning bathroom—well, sort of functioning. Privacy was an issue. Because of construction, a gaping hole had been cut in the bathroom floor. Right next to the throne seat. One morning, one of us (I won't say which one) was enjoying the benefit of some quiet time on the throne when suddenly two hardhats appeared up through the hole in the floor. The workmen had arrived early. It made for an awkward moment, but became part of the fun and adventure.

We were located on a half-acre of land, but backed onto three hundred acres of forest complete with hiking trails. We walked. We skied. We raised rabbits, mice, rats, turtles, snakes, hedgehogs, and three litters of beautiful Siberian husky pups. You name it, we raised it. We lived across from a farm and helped deliver calves and round up cattle. We saw lots of wildlife in our backyard: fox, coyotes, deer. And one day, we encountered a bull. Yes, a big black bull with long horns and snorting nostrils. He was just standing there daring anyone to throw a red flag in front of him. We tried to lasso him with a rope, but the rope tangled on one of his horns. You don't want to know the rest of the story. One year, we built a fire pit amongst the trees and spent many evenings around a fire roasting hot dogs and marshmallows, that is until the mosquitoes drove us inside.

My son Jeremy and I spent many days cutting down trees to open up our house to the sun. A lot of the wood was cut up and piled for burning at the family altar, our indispensable, venerated woodstove. It was an invaluable time for our family. For me, the whole experience was therapeutic and a wonderful diversion from the stresses of ministry. Many friends joined us in the adventure, and we developed many wonderful and lasting relationships. It is amazing how the community of faith—friends—come around and help carry the burden of the weak. We were the weak, and I will never forget those days.

The area where we were living was called Bethesda. We put up a sign at the end of the driveway that proclaimed it "Our Bethesda." Bethesda is the name of a place in the Bible, and it means "place of healing." Perfect name. This was our place of healing. God's provision.

Things began to heat up considerably in the church as my contractual term came to an end at the college and seminary. The leadership of the church had asked me to return full-time as their pastor. We really believed God had called us to this church and community and that He had not lifted that call. So, with some fear and trepidation, we agreed to return full-time. The leaders decided to hold a confirmation vote. They saw no problem and felt this would be a way to consolidate the church behind me and the leadership.

It backfired! What they misjudged was the exploitation of the telephone and the depth of animosity. The few dissenters were busy on the phone that week informing everyone of the reasons why I should not be coming back. I was painted in very dark, foreboding, and menacing colours, and they were successful in dissuading the people from the wishes of their elders. I was voted out! I will never forget that night. Diane and I were numb. We drove home to our Bethesda—and sat, staring. We hadn't seen this coming. What were we to do now? How do we tell the kids? How do we protect them from hurt? How do we keep them from anger?

The church went into shock. That week was one of the most distressing weeks in our lives. Countless phone calls. Visits. Tears. Friends came around us. Comforting. Hurt. Angry. Stupefied. It was like one long wake. The pain we felt in our souls was acute. We could feel the severe penetrating pain of our flock. And we were not able to offer much comfort. For the first time, I was their pastor and could not help them. But no, I was not their pastor. They were pastorless, and I was flockless.

The spiritual battle was obvious and intense. Darkness held the church hostage. The church leadership called me one morning and informed me that they were gathering for prayer and asked if I would like to join them. I did. It was one of the most overwhelming prayer meetings I have ever participated in. Little was said. Just silence. Each man quietly wept. There was brokenness. There was a keen sense of the Spirit's presence like I had never felt before. We were on holy ground. Some of the best praying you can do is without words. You don't know where to start. You don't know what to say. You just kneel silently before the Lord and let the Holy Spirit pray for you. He knows your heart's cry, and He knows what the will of the Father is. He marvelously brings the two together. That's what we did that morning. And it broke the bondage. We were not without intense struggle in the months ahead.

But Diane and I returned to pastoral ministry. And we have been here at the same church for twenty-five years now.

The turn of events that God used to return us to the church unleashed severe spiritual and emotional attacks on my character, integrity, and motives. The emotional abuse, slander, and malice were turned up another degree. Threats were made, demanding my resignation. It was difficult to know how to respond. Why the intensity? Why such a degree of hostility? Those questions persist to this day. One letter warned me that if I didn't take some years away from ministry and exhibit some very painful honesty and humbling, a terrible disaster would befall me and others close to me in the very near future. This was not the first time such threatening words had been spoken. One day a woman sat in our living room and told me God had sent her to tell me there was sin in my life and that if I did not repent and change, I would lose one of my children very soon. I asked her what the sin was, and she informed me that God had not told her. Didn't sound much like something God would say or do. But these things can be disconcerting. One must be careful to discern the voices. God has not given us the spirit of fear.

GETTING AWAY

It's probably not surprising that at the end of those few intense years, I was spiritually and emotionally depleted. Emptied. Bled. That summer, our family decided to take a trip out west to the Rockies. This would be a great time for our family, and we all looked forward to it with great anticipation. Lots of planning went into it. We got the maps out on the floor and charted the route. We planned to go west following the Trans-Canada, wind our way through the mountains, and pay a visit to Vancouver Island. We would then make our way home following the route through the USA. God had provided us with a full-size van. We could load it up with all the food, apparatus, and gear we needed as well as haul a small camper along behind us.

I can still remember the day we headed off. A full month of travel and family time. We all had our roles to play. We had setup and take-down to a science. As dinner was being prepared on the camp stove, the camper was erected, firewood gathered and split, and drinking water hauled from a central tap. After supper, we would explore the vicinity around our campsite. It was one of the highlights of life. We weren't too many kilometres down the road before I had left the problems behind. Well, sort of. It was hard to shake everything loose. But I was determined to leave it behind and just enjoy my family. Actually, I was running. Not from God. I owed my life and health to Him. Running from people. From church. From problems. From anything. I was outta there. Coming home? Didn't want to think about that. That was a month down the road. I just needed to be away. North Superior. The prairies. The Rockies. The Pacific. It was everything we expected and more.

On the return trip, there was one particular place I wanted to visit. The historical site of the Battle of the Little Bighorn. The place where George Armstrong Custer and his famed Seventh Cavalry encountered Sioux warriors one hot June day in 1876 in a battle that was the bloody climax to one of the most remarkable sagas in American history. More than 260 soldiers, including Custer, met stunning defeat and death at the hands of several thousand Sioux and Cheyenne warriors under the outstanding leadership of chiefs Sitting Bull and Crazy Horse. We travelled through the beautiful Glacier International Park. Elk and deer wandered across the road. Regal bighorn sheep and white wooly mountain goats peered down from their lofty peaks. We hiked along threadlike paths on the steep mountainsides of the Continental Divide, some of the most breathtaking scenery in the world. And then we descended into the rolling hills of Montana, miles and miles of endless prairie grass and boundless sky. Antelope played on the ridges. A graceful doe followed a stream deep in a hollow with three, yes, three fawns trailing along behind her. She and her triplets took time to stop and give us a long, curious gaze.

That Sunday morning when we started out, Diane shared how nice it would be to go to church somewhere as a family. This was the first time she had mentioned anything like this. I looked over at her and gave a polite nod. I felt a cold chill go through me. Her innocent comment brought back a flood of feelings that were just too painful. Church was the last place I wanted to be. My life was the church. This was time apart. Away. I tried to make a humorous comment in return. "Sure, but I don't see a church anywhere out here, do you? Just prairie and sky. Guess we'll have to settle for yellow grass and a clear blue sky." There was nothing funny about my response. I guessed my sentiments were showing. She turned her head toward the side window and stared in the other direction. There was an awkward silence.

THE BATTLE AT BIGHORN

We drove all day. The sun was low in the west, and its rays cast a blinding glare over the roadside sign indicating our nearness to the Little Bighorn Battlefield National Monument. A few miles to go. And then another sign, Crow Native Reserve. We kept our eyes peeled for an appropriate place to camp for the night. We would tour the battlefield the next morning. Over to the left in the middle of a wide field, we spotted a large domelike structure with flashing, revolving lights and a sign that could be seen a hundred miles away. Casino. You couldn't miss it. It stood out unabashedly like a giant Goliath, its armour glistening in the rays of the setting sun. Just a quarter mile farther, in the shadow of this bombastic behemoth, was a tent. It was proportionally much smaller than the casino, but it was large enough to hold a hundred or so people. There was no doubt about the purpose of the tent. It stood there poised with the humble defiance of a David, lowly slingshot in hand but armed with the name of the living God. Above it was a large banner with the words, *REVIVAL MEETINGS.* Diane blurted out, "There's our church!" I was snared.

We found our campsite and after a family discussion, it was decided we would investigate the tent meeting. I didn't have much choice. So off we set. The tent was encircled by old beat-up half-tons. People were seated inside the truck cabs, posted like sentinels on the tops of the cabs, crowded into the trailer boxes, and perched on the bumpers. The sound of guitars and drums and lively singing reverberated from under the canvas ceiling. The tent was filled with the commotion of people crammed into a confined space and the constant clamour of children talking and crying. I looked for an inconspicuous place to sit down. The only chairs I could spot were along the back row right against the rear canvas wall. We tried to slip in as unnoticeably as we could. Actually, in a crowded tent of dark-skinned Crow Indians, we were about as inconspicuous as light bulbs in a dark room. We sat down. Everyone knew we were there.

From what I could tell, the meeting was being led by four Crow pastors. They led the worship, played the instruments, prayed, shared the gospel, and preached the messages with passion and fervency. There were several messages preached. Each with increased zeal. We had arrived about 8:30 PM. The tent meeting had been going on for three or four hours before we had arrived, and it was now several hours since our arrival. And it seemed things were just warming up. It was a sultry summer night, and the temperature in the tent was rising. Little did I realize just how warm it was going to get.

Everyone under the canvas roof began to sing as if on cue, "We are standing on holy ground … we are standing in His presence on holy ground."[1] We were thinking we should get going because of the time. As the song began to wind down, one of the native pastors got up onto the makeshift platform and turned to Romans 8. We thought this might be the best time to make our exit. Just as I leaned forward to signal to the kids that we should go now, I heard the preacher bellow, "I don't know what you're running from!"

Have you ever known a time when someone pressed the pause button on your life? When words were spoken publicly but seemed to be aimed directly at you? One of those moments when you felt like you were under surveillance on the end of someone's telescope? I looked up, and he was pointing straight at me. The colour drained from my face.

It got worse. He stepped down off of the platform and started to walk toward me, his boney finger still pointed at me like an arrow flying my direction. I sat upright in my chair. My head was pressed against the back of the canvas. I had nowhere to go. Trapped. Ambushed. Have you ever known a time when you felt like God was stalking you? I had come to the Little Bighorn to enjoy and explore the location of the last great battle of the American west, not to fight my own battles. Not to be engaged in a spiritual conflict that boiled inside of me. Here I was in the middle of Montana, in the middle of the American west, in what seemed like the middle of nowhere, and far from home. And I was ambushed by God.

When the preacher was about ten feet away, he spoke in a passionate but penetrating voice, "I don't know what you've done, or what you're running from." By now every eye was focused on me. Diane and my kids were looking at me with a somewhat frantic look in their eyes. I could read in everyone's faces, "What has he done?" I wanted to shout out, "I'm innocent! I've done nothing!" But I was paralyzed. I felt like a serial killer. At least, I imagined that that's what everyone else was envisioning. A certain uneasiness, a sense of alarm entered my being. I knew what had happened to the last white guy who was in this situation on this same land one hundred plus years earlier!

FROM CHAPTER 19 TO CHAPTER 8

The preacher used his one hand to point and the other to grip his Bible. He glanced from me to his Bible for a brief instant. I felt a sudden split-second of relief from the focused stare of my assailant who had relentlessly pursued me since leaving the cover of his pulpit. The relief dissipated just as quickly as his eyes rebounded back to me. He embarked on a series of questions, all straight out of Romans 8. "If God is for you, who can ever be against you?"

I shook my head to signify no one. I knew that was the answer he wanted. I had decided under the circumstances, my best plan of retreat would be agreement. The karate technique: go with the throw.

He continued his pursuit. He looked at his Bible again and then straight back at me. The back of my head was pressed as hard as it could be against the tent wall. Diane's eyes were as big as saucers. My kids looked traumatized.

"If God did not spare even His own Son but gave Him up for you, won't He meet every other need that you have?"

"Yes, He can … or, er, w– will," I stuttered.

"Do you feel accused by man?" he asked.

"Yes, I do," I answered back, though rather timidly. But it was as though the preacher had opened a door and invited me in. He had entered my space uninvited, so I decided to enter his space and dialogue with this messenger from heaven. My heart began to open up. "Yes, I do feel accused," I refuted. "In fact, I have been maliciously accused. Maligned. Unfairly. Unjustly. I'm tired. Wiped. Done."

"Who dares accuse you whom God has chosen for His own?" he questioned. "No one," he retorted, before I could get an answer in. "For God has given you right standing with Himself. So what if men accuse you? Let them! What matters is that you belong to God. What matters is that you are in right standing with God.

"Who will condemn you?" he asked, soliciting a reply from me.

"No one!" I said with more passion than I had felt in a long time.

"That's right," he replied. "Because Jesus died for you, was raised for you, and prays in heaven for you. Just think of that!

"Now, tell me." His voice lowered and softened, as though reaching right down into my heart. "Think of everything that Christ has done for you because He loves you. When you experience trouble and accusation and threat and oppression, does that mean that Jesus has stopped loving you?" The room was packed beyond capacity and every eye was glued to the preacher and his prey. But it was as though we were alone in the room. Just this native preacher and me, or maybe I should say, just God and me.

Tears began to fill my eyes. The face in front of me became glazed. His auburn-skinned countenance seemed to be the face of an angel. The tears washed my eyes, but even more, my heart, for they flowed from my heart.

The man leaned down and placed his coarse, high cheekbone against the side of my head. "Can anything ever separate you from Christ's love?" he whispered in my ear.

"No … nothing," I said.

"Then there is nothing and no one to run from, only Someone to run to," he responded tenderly. "You are in His hands, His care, and His love. Be strong and courageous."

There was no uncertainty that God had met me at the wall. He will often meet you in chapter 19 of your life. That's where I was. But my encounter with God led me to chapter 8: a divine appointment, in a most unexpected way, in a most unlikely place, by a most unusual messenger.

I had been standing in His presence on holy ground. When you hit the wall, tread carefully, stand silently, and listen attentively. You may be in His presence. On holy ground.

Rose's Story

I felt a lump in my breast. Initially, I chose to discount it because cancer was not in my family history. But I knew I could not ignore it and made an appointment with my doctor. The diagnosis was a shock even though I thought I had prepared myself for the worst. Cancer.

I began to experience an emotional roller coaster. There were good days and bad days. My emotional pendulum would swing from feeling relatively strong to feeling absolutely weak. From sheer joy to complete despondency. All the tests began to drain my energy. And the pain … the pain was more than you would think anyone could possibly endure. But endure I did.

After my second surgery, I encountered a devastating moment. I was standing in front of my bedroom mirror removing the bandages. As I watched the unmasking of my surgical wounds, the true character of my disease was exposed. I saw my chest for the first time since the surgery. I wept. I knew from that moment I would never be the same again. I was not only scarred, I was seriously disfigured for the rest of my life. At that point I became more self-conscious than I had ever been before. I wept uncontrollably.

Chemo was another low point. Six treatments. My hair fell out and weakness set in. Following each treatment there were two days when I was so weak I found myself wishing for death just to get it over with. During these lowest of times, all I could do was sleep, getting up only to go to the bathroom. I felt like such a failure. I could not care for my family let alone myself. A question kept ringing in my head, "God, what are You saying to me?"

My friend Tracy was always there for me whenever I called, and even when I didn't call. Every day, she would contact me or drop by, coffee in hand, with a cheery face and a positive attitude. One night, she picked me up for a ladies' night out. I had just completed my second chemo treatment and had shaved my head a couple of days previous. I was feeling dispirited and that day had crocheted a hat under which to hide my head. Arriving at the restaurant, I took my coat off, and we sat down at a table and prepared to order dinner. Tracy sat across from me still wearing her jacket, scarf, and hood. It was February, but it wasn't that chilly in the restaurant. "Are you cold?" I asked. She smirked and removed her hood. I was speechless. Her head had been shaved. I suddenly felt a bond with her I had never experienced before. I removed my own hat. We stared at each other, smiled, and then tears filled our eyes. The rest of the evening was spent laughing and giggling like a couple of schoolgirls. All my self-consciousness had evaporated. Two bald-headed, middle-aged women grinning from ear to ear. Priceless.

11 Finding Friends at the Wall

Someone has said, "Sometimes angels don't have wings; they're called 'friends.'" I would have to agree.

I was recently inspired by the life story of the abolitionist William Wilberforce. One of the things that struck me was the impact of friends in his life. I was particularly impressed by friendships that came together and surrounded Wilberforce to bring the slave trade to an end in the British Empire. While Wilberforce carries the honour for abolishing the slave trade, in reality, it was a handful of friends with him who accomplished this colossal undertaking. It would not have occurred without them. Over the exhaustive, strenuous twenty years of debating, friends were as essential to Wilberforce as the majority vote in the House of Commons on the night of February 23, 1807, that abolished the slave trade.

There was Isaac Milner, renowned as a Cambridge tutor, one of the new "evangelicals," and a man of great intellect. Wilberforce was fascinated by Milner's blend of intellect and faith. He invited Milner along with him on a vacation to France with the purpose of picking his brain regarding the teachings of Christianity. That vacation was to prove to be a life-changing episode in Wilberforce's journey. Christianity seemed to be so rich in meaning in contrast to his own life that seemed increasingly shallow. Milner was influential in Wilberforce surrendering his life to Christ.

There was William Pitt. Pitt was the prime minister of England, and while not a friend who encouraged Wilberforce in his faith, nonetheless he was a very close friend and ally in the abolitionist movement. Talk about having friends in high places.

Then there was William Cowper, Wilberforce's favourite poet. Henry Thorton, his cousin. And his close friend, Edward Eliot, whom he could always count on for encouragement and in whom he could always confide.

Wilberforce had another special friend and mentor, John Newton, the former slave captain who later composed the well-known hymn *Amazing Grace*. Newton was considered a fanatic by London society, and Wilberforce risked ridicule by entering Newton's door. But it was Newton who gave him rich pastoral counsel and encouraged the young Wilberforce to nurture his faith and remain in politics. In 1786, Wilberforce had experienced a great change in his life after coming to faith in Christ. But he also hit a spiritual wall of doubt regarding his call in life. There were times when he considered leaving the political arena because he could not reconcile his Christian faith with his career. Could a Christian really be a politician? Yes, said Newton. Not only a politician, but a good one. Could one be engaged in the politics of the day and still remain faithful to God? Yes, advised Newton. Was that not the Daniel of the Bible?

Wilberforce hit a physical wall. He was often gravely ill, beleaguered by a weak physical frame. He hit a twenty-year political wall of continual setback, disappointment, opposition, slander, and threats of personal violence. And then there was the tyranny of an oppressive emotional wall. Dashed hopes and anxiety culminated in several nervous breakdowns. It was those times when Wilberforce questioned whether he was the right man to champion the abolitionist cause that his friends assured him that he was. No doubt! When discouragement and even despair set in, his friends would rally around him. When ridicule and threat harassed him, his friends stood beside him. When the task overwhelmed him, his friends supported him and encouraged him to stay the course.

In 1796, Wilberforce suffered his second emotional breakdown. Considering a retreat from public life, he communicated to his friend and mentor John Newton his reluctance to go on. Newton replied with a letter that was pivotal in Wilberforce's life and the abolitionist cause.

> You are not only a representative for Yorkshire, you have the far greater honour of being a representative for the Lord, in a place where many know Him not, and an opportunity of showing them what are the genuine fruits of that religion which you are known to profess…
>
> It is true that you live in the midst of difficulties and snares, and you need a double guard of watchfulness and prayer. But since you know both your need of help, and where to look for it, I may say to you as Darius to Daniel, "Thy God whom thou servest continually is able to preserve and deliver you."
>
> … The promise, "My grace is sufficient for thee," is necessary to support us in the smoothest scenes, and is equally able to support us in the most difficult.
>
> … He is always near. He knows our wants, our dangers, our feeling, and our fears. By looking to Him we are enlightened and made strong out of weakness.[1]

What an encouragement! What a friend! When you hit the wall, you need a friend.

THE RISK OF FRIENDSHIP

I believe in friends. And I have some very good friends. I must admit, however, that I have struggled with friendship. As a pastor I have befriended people only to have that friendship soiled by something. Several times, it has been a betrayal of trust. I have shared things in confidence only to have that confidence betrayed and misrepresented. That's a hard one to get over. In fact it can build a wall of paranoia around you that shields you from a true friendship. Sometimes, I discovered that the friendship was conditional. I would just begin to develop a trust when I discovered that the friendship was conditional upon me making pastoral or administrative decisions that were in agreement with the opinions of my "friend."

Time is another factor. Friendship involves making the time to invest in the friendship. The logic is simple. Your life is busy. Time is restricted and precious. You invest the time, however, to nurture a good friendship. The friendship grows. The friendship fails. The valuable time is lost.

Then there are those people who warm up to you and want to be your friend but prove to be what I have heard H. B. London call "joy suckers." They suck the joy, life, and energy right out of you. They are not the kind of person who is going to come alongside you and energize you in your time of need. These are often people who want you as a friend because they need you and that's where it ends. The word *parasite* comes to mind. The word comes from the Greek and means literally "beside the wheat." It is a little creature that sits beside the wheat and eats it. I'm thinking of the person who eats off of you, who lives off of you. They take but don't give. Drain but don't replenish. Benefit from but don't reciprocate. Suck but don't restore. These are needy people and need help but are not the kind of friend I speak of.

Despite these perils, however, it is necessary to find friends and to be a friend. Friendship has a risk factor. But it is worth the risk. If friendship has failed you, it is worth trying again. You'll need it when you hit the wall.

JESUS' FRIENDS

When I think of friendship, I think of Jesus. One of the first things He did when He began His ministry was to call disciples, or *talmidim. Talmidim* were students of a rabbi who dedicated themselves to learning from the rabbi and to becoming just like him. But Jesus also called them His friends. They were to become each other's friends as well. The word Jesus would have used was *haverim.* A *haver* was a friend and fellow student. *Haverim* (the plural form of the word) spent time together, studied together, learned together, discussed and debated the Scriptures together, refined each other. The relationship went beyond superficial words to relating in deeper, more meaningful ways.

Lois Tverberg shares relevant practical insight into the relationship between *haverim.*

> A *haver* is like a spiritual 'jogging partner'—someone for whom you'll crawl out of bed on a rainy morning, putting on

> your running shoes instead of hitting the snooze button. Once you're up and running together, your pace is a little faster, you keep going a little longer. You are pushed intellectually and spiritually. If we really want to mature in faith and as disciples, we need to develop relationships that force us to grow, by getting ourselves some *haverim.*[2]

Among Jesus' *haverim* were three we might call His special friends. Peter, James, and John. In the midst of need, Jesus often retreated to some quiet spot with this inner circle of friends. I'm not sure what they always talked about, but He shared with them, and they encouraged and supported each other.

On the night before Jesus' crucifixion, Jesus led His *talmidim* down the steep path just outside Jerusalem's southern wall, across the Brook Kidron and into a garden called Gethsemane. Gethsemane means "olive press." It was a place Jesus liked to go. Quiet. Away from the bustle of the Jerusalem streets. A place to meditate. A place to pray. This was the night. The agony of crucifixion lay ahead. The spiritual torment of carrying in His sinless person the weight of the slime of every sin ever committed. Lying. Pride. Jealousy. Murder. Pedophilia. Everything. The unparalleled anguish of being abandoned by His Father in heaven, a Father who was unable to look upon the filth that would saturate Jesus' pure being. Such anguish Jesus had never experienced. He had hit the wall. And He wanted His friends with Him.

He took Peter, James, and John with Him, *"and he became anguished and distressed. He told them, 'My soul is crushed with grief to the point of death. Stay here and keep watch with me'"* (Matthew 26:37–38). Jesus then went on alone a little farther into the garden and fell to the ground. I can't help but imagine that He went to the place where the olive press stood. He was familiar with the process of producing olive oil. The olives were dumped into a large stone bowl called a sea. A millstone was attached to a donkey by a pole and the animal would circle the sea moving the millstone over the olives, cracking them and crushing them into mush. The olives were then scooped up and poured into burlap bags. For phase two in the process, the bags were carried to the olive press. The press was a heavy stone pillar that was lowered onto the burlap bags. As the weight of the stone pillar pressed down on the olives, the rich red olive oil began to ooze from the olives and run down a channel into containers.

I can see Jesus falling to His knees, reaching up His hand and gripping the great stone pillar of the olive press and crying, *"My soul is crushed with grief to the point of death."* The olive is Jesus and the flesh of the olive is broken as the weight of the olive press, the *gethsemane*—our sin—presses down upon Him. Luke wrote, *"He was in such agony of spirit that his sweat fell to the ground like great drops of blood"* (Luke 22:44). The blood of the broken olive, His flesh, began to run and would within a few hours drain from His body down the shaft of a cross like a conduit to touch the life of everyone who would believe.

He prayed that this cup of suffering might be removed. But then He added that His Father's will should be done and not His own. There was no other way. He had hit the great wall. And He needed His friends. He needed their companionship, their attention to what was occurring, their support, watchfulness, and prayer. Three times He returned to them. Three times they were sleeping. They let Him down. So God sent an angel to strengthen Him and keep Him company. Too bad they didn't fulfill that need. But if Jesus needed friends in His hour of need, how much more do we?

STICKY FRIENDS

Solomon, the wisest man who ever lived, wrote, *"A real friend sticks closer than a brother"* (Proverbs 18:24). He also wrote, *"A friend is always loyal, and a brother is born to help in time of need"* (Proverbs 17:17). When I hit my first major wall and I was feeling the rejection of most people, there were two guys who became my friends. They weren't leaders in the church. They weren't men who stood out in any significant way. They weren't the kind who would have been asked to be an elder in the church. They were two who struggled with having to slip outside for a cigarette. They weren't who I would have expected to come alongside. But, in fact, they were far more than I expected.

Gord had a small farm on the outskirts of town. He and his wife had welcomed a bag lady into their home just because they had compassion for her. And now he welcomed me into his life. We often met for coffee. He didn't have much to share with me from the Bible, but he sure lived it. He told me, "I want to be your friend." He meant more to me than he will ever know.

My other friend was Darrell. I got a job welding for a short while. And Darrell worked in the same welding shop. He was a young Christian. Every day he came alongside to encourage me. To speak into my life. He taught me how to weld. In fact, I ended up working with him every day. We encouraged each other in our lives. Some of the best encouragement I ever received came from Darrell while welding a steel seam under the frame of a giant Mack truck.

When I hit the second major wall in my life some years later, my deepest source of hurt sprang from the betrayal of people who had called themselves friends. But God placed someone else in my life. Someone I had known for a long time. I have heard it said that the deepest friendships come from those who were your friends during your college years and before. Those who knew you when growing up. The ones you hung out with in the earlier years. This was one of those friends. We grew through our teen years together. Bruce was now the president of a Bible college and seminary. He had inherited a significant financial crisis that consumed most of his time and had a need for someone to assist him. And so with his need and in my need, he came to me and asked me to take on a one-year contract position at the college, assisting him in the area of human resources. That's good, strong mutual friendship. I did it. I continued the teaching role at the church. I served at the college and seminary, assisting the president. I did some teaching at the college. It was the change I needed. The diversion I needed. And the friend I needed.

True friends are loyal. You can count on them. They'll stick to you, even when you've done wrong. They know all the yucky stuff, and they still love and accept you. Even when you are wearing your poker face, they can read your eyes, and they know when you are hurting. They have your best interests in mind. They seem to know just what you need to hear, and they have the courage to speak into your life. I like the lyrics of the song *You've Got a Friend* by Carole King. Whatever the season is that you're going through, "All you've to do is call, and I'll be there, yes, I will."[3] A true friend shows up.

TWO BEST FRIENDS

The two best friends in the Bible were David and Jonathan, a most unlikely pair. David was chosen by God to be the next king of Israel. Jonathan was the son of the present king, Saul. That means Jonathan had everything to lose. He would have been next in line to the throne. He could have been jealous. Embittered. Instead, he befriended David. And he did not just befriend David; they became best friends.

Jonathan understood and submitted to the will of his God. He acquired an unswerving, uncompromising loyalty to David. When David hit the wall and had to flee the jealous rage of Jonathan's father, King Saul, Jonathan risked his life for David. And David entrusted his life to Jonathan. What a friendship. David could call Jonathan's name at any time, and Jonathan would come running. That's a friend.

A TRUE FRIEND

Solomon, David's son, wrote a book called Ecclesiastes. Solomon had everything a human being could have in this world. And yet I wonder how often he felt alone and without a friend. I sense that fact when he bemoans the condition of a man who has gained much wealth but feels so alone. He calls it meaningless and depressing (Ecclesiastes 4:7–8). Then he talks about the advantages of companionship and gives us some great attributes of a true friend.

HORSEPOWER

"Two people are better off than one, for they can help each other succeed" (Ecclesiastes 4:9). This is called synergy. *Synergy* means that the total output of a team is greater than the sum of the outputs of each person working independently. For example, one draft horse can pull four tons. But two draft horses can pull much more than twice the weight of what the one can pull. Two can pull an astonishing twenty-two tons. That's synergy.

The early pioneers discovered that they could build many more barns in a year by bringing the whole community together rather than by leaving each farmer to himself to build his own barn. So they held frequent barn-raising bees. A farmer left to himself might never get the job done. Together, the farmers could construct a barn in one or two days.

A friend can be a huge help in your life. Especially when you hit the wall. Your chance of success, of prevailing through the challenge, of getting through the struggle, is many times greater with a friend than alone.

I'LL BE THERE, YES I WILL

Solomon continues, *"If one person falls, the other can reach out and help. But someone who falls alone is in real trouble"* (Ecclesiastes 4:10). Imagine you're backpacking in the wilderness and you fall and break your leg. Your chance of survival may depend on whether you are alone or have a companion. When you hit an emotional or spiritual wall, many people will not understand the dilemma. Many people respond to what they can see or understand. A broken spirit is harder to see or understand than a broken leg. A true friend will discern and help.

Galatians 6:1–2 states, *"If any believer is overcome by some sin, you who are godly should gently and humbly help that person back onto the right path … Share each other's burdens."* The word *help* or *restore* is the word for mending a broken bone. A friend not only forgives, but is prepared to restore you to health. A friend will bandage your wounds, quench your thirst, and help you back onto your feet. Whatever it takes, they are there for you.

I remember hearing a story some time ago that goes back to the Vietnam War. Refugees were fleeing Vietnam by the hundreds and thousands. Desperate people streamed along the roads. One reporter spotted a young girl carrying a large bundle on her back. Upon closer inspection, he discovered it to be a little boy. The reporter exclaimed, "He must be heavy!" She looked up at him and responded, "He ain't heavy; he's my brother."

When you fall, a true friend will pick you up. He or she will carry you. You are never too heavy. Love and loyalty can carry a heavy load. Jesus said, *"There is no greater love than to lay down one's life for one's friends"* (John 15:13). Love is an action word. Here it means to do whatever it takes to help your friend back up. Just as Jesus laid down His life for His friends to pull us through to safety, a true friend will pull you through, whatever the cost.

BREATHING LIFE

Solomon continues in Ecclesiastes 4:11: *"Likewise, two people lying close together can keep each other warm. But how can one be warm alone?" Webster's Dictionary* defines *warm* as "giving out heat." But I think we can apply this to more than the energy created by the random motion of molecules in a body. *Webster's* also defines warmth as "infusing with a feeling of love, friendship and well-being … to fill with passion." Warmth is life. When warmth is infused, life is restored. Warmth means to inspire or breathe life into someone. To speak life into a person. To ignite someone to action, hope, or perseverance. It means to fill someone with the passion to start living again. We speak of warming up before a game. One exercises to limber up, to get the blood circulating. A friend provides the warm-up that readies you for living, for getting back in the game.

We are like embers from a fire. When you take a stick and separate the embers from each other, they slowly die. But when you heap them back together, the heat of one ignites the other.

Solomon put it another way in Proverbs 27:17. *"As iron sharpens iron, so a friend sharpens a friend."* A friend sharpens and warms by his or her presence. You can't shake them. They hold on. A friend adds another perspective. Tells you the hard stuff. Challenges your thinking. Holds you accountable. Adds some good humour. A little comic relief. It is good to have a friend who makes you laugh. Who keeps you from taking life so seriously that you seize up. Who helps you to switch from low gear into a higher gear. A true friend knows how to drop healing words at just the right time. *"Kind words are like honey—sweet to the soul and healthy for the body"* (Proverbs 16:24).

I have a brother who is also a good friend. Recently, I led our church through some significant changes. Did I just say "change"? Yes, change. Change usually unsettles the security of some, and one day someone walked into my office and unloaded an attack on my motives. It has always amazed me how people think they are masters of discerning motives and run around like the motive police, challenging what they believe is your reason for doing what you do. There are often some charges laid against your character. Well, this was one of those times.

The next day, I found a card on my desk. It was from my brother. It read,

> When I was a young cop many years ago, I was on the stand giving evidence. Upon cross-examination, the defense lawyer went up one side of me and down the other. When I returned to my seat, feeling defeated about having just lost the whole case, the crown prosecutor looked at me and remarked, "That's good news … they don't have a case. We're going to win this one." I was a bit confused by his response and when I questioned him why, he responded that when they go after your character that means that they have no case … that's the only thing they can go after. Ring a bell? The devil sifts us like wheat when he feels threatened. That could be happening here! But this will pass. For now, put your feet up, read a good book, and move on. Signed, Roger.

That's infusing warmth and inspiring life.

About the same time, another friend, an elder in the church, e-mailed me with this encouraging note. "Thank you for your determination, courage and yes, sheer guts, for defending the church you love and that belongs to our Lord Jesus! He will surely bless us and provide all we need. We can and will trust in Him!! Thank you for being my pastor and friend. We love you." Signed, Ron. That's infusing warmth and inspiring life.

WATCHING YOUR BACK

There's one more thing Solomon says about true friendship. *"A person standing alone can be attacked and defeated, but two can stand back-to-back and conquer"* (Ecclesiastes 4:12). There is strength in numbers. A good friend covers your back. Protects you.

When I lived in that special part of God's creation, Northern Ontario, I remember witnessing the herds of whitetail deer congregate every year at the same time. It was the late fall, just as the snow began to fall. The herds were called deer yards. It was not uncommon in some locations to spot forty to fifty deer yarded up among the conifer stands for the winter. One of the primary reasons deer do this is for protection. There is safety in numbers. Gathering together or herding minimizes the danger of wolf attack in the winter versus standing and running alone. The musk ox is another animal that lives in the far north and travels in a herd. When the herd is threatened, musk oxen have an effective way of defending themselves. The bulls and cows all face outward toward the predator, forming a protective ring around the calves. The defensive instincts of these animals give us an illustration of what Solomon was thinking when he wrote, "*A person standing alone can be attacked and defeated, but two can stand back-to-back and conquer.*" He added, *"Three are even better"* (verse 12).

Our history has produced many wise leaders who stood out in their times. None were more brilliant than the Shawnee chief Tecumseh. The site of his death at the Battle of the Thames in 1813 is not far from our home. He was a man of intellect, charisma, and wisdom, and he used his influence to weld together an Indian confederacy such as had never been witnessed before or since. Tecumseh brought tribes together that for decades had been sworn enemies, in an attempt to arrest the white man's westward expansion over Indian lands, reducing his people to a mere shadow of what they had once proudly been. Tecumseh understood the principle cited by Solomon. In 1799, at a council of about seventy Wyandots and Ottawas, he touched their souls deeply with typical native imagery. "Any child can snap with ease the single hair from a horse's tail, but not the strongest man, nor the wildest stallion, can break the rope woven of these same hairs."[4] This is exactly what Solomon was saying. There is strength and protection in numbers.

On another occasion, Tecumseh, speaking to his fellow chiefs, said, "Now we are weak and many of our people are afraid. But hear me; a single twig breaks, but the bundle of twigs is strong. Someday I will embrace our brother tribes and draw them into a bundle and together we will win our country back from the whites."[5] He almost succeeded.

When you face an invincible wall, it is not wise to be alone. The devil would love to get you alone to attack and devour you. The world can easily suck you into its seductive pull. It is often when you are down and alone that people will turn against you. Hitting the wall is a juncture when you may even turn on yourself. Believe it or not, this is a time ripe for self-blame. Deep discouragement. Dangerous compromise. The beginning of an unending cycle of self-abasement. You need someone to encourage you. Keep you strong. Warn you of danger. Help you make wise choices. Hold you accountable. Watch out for you in your moment of woundedness, confusion, or fear. A friend to cover your back.

HOLD!

We have a photo hanging in our home. I took the picture when we were at Miletus in western Turkey, just down the road from the excavated city of Ephesus. Miletus is one of the ancient sites visited by the apostle Paul. The picture was taken in the ruins of the old first-century arena in Miletus. The shot looks up an old flight of stone stairs that opens at the top out into the arena. When I look at that picture, I wonder what it must have been like for poor captives, slaves, or political prisoners being herded up those stairs with no idea of what awaited them at the top. Listening to the deafening roar of the crowd calling for blood. Their blood. Or for gladiators, often victims themselves, wondering if this was their hour to die as a sacrifice to satisfy the appetite of the bloodthirsty mob.

The movie *Gladiator* is the story of one such gladiator.[6] The powerful general Maximus Decimus Meridius is betrayed and forced into slavery. He trains as a gladiator and rises through the gladiatorial ranks to avenge the murder of his wife and son and his Emperor Aurelius. For me, the climax in the story is when Maximus and his fellow gladiators ascend the stone stairway out into the arena. They stand as though hypnotized in the middle of the arena floor, their eyes and ears transfixed on the throngs crying for their brutal death. They had hit their wall.

Their attention turns toward the iron gates on the circumference of the arena floor, apprehensive of the unknown and anticipating the worst. They have no idea what will burst from those gates. They know only that whatever spews, it will be fashioned for their bloody demise. Maximus speaks calmly but with resolve and intention. "Whatever comes out of these gates, we've got a better chance of survival if we work together ... we stay together, we survive."[7]

Suddenly, it happens. The gates swing open. The masses send up a chilling cheer as horses pulling war chariots emerge out the dark passageways from behind the doors on all sides. Knives protrude from the wheels of the chariots, flashing with each rotation. A driver snaps a whip at the horses, and a fighter wields his bow and short spear. The horses pound the dirt with their hoofs as they charge toward the paltry-looking cluster of men in the centre of the field. The drivers then make a wide sweep around the clustered gladiators as though encircling their prey.

The charioteers charge. Arrows fill the air. Shields are lifted. Dust swirls. Some of the gladiators panic. The tiny compact unit begins to fragment. A few break rank. Isolated, they quickly fall victim to the strike of an arrow and the blow of a spear. They are trampled under the deadly hoofs. Midst the confusion and chaos the voice of Maximus can be heard. "Come together! Come together!" The rest begin to pull back. They remember the words of their leader, "We stay together, we survive." They recoil into a back-to-back position. Shields are tightly pressed together. Maximus commands, "Hold! Hold!" The savage onslaught persists. Wave after wave. But the call goes out again and again, "Hold! Hold!" And they do. They hold.[8]

None of us know what we will face in life. But whatever wall you face, you will need a friend who will instill courage, inspire hope, and infuse strength. A friend who will stand back-to-back with you and encourage you to hold. A Maximus. He is the kind of friend I would want with me when I need someone to watch my back.

BEING A FRIEND

By the way, everything I have just said about finding a friend at the wall? It applies to you *being* a friend to someone else. The best way to find a true friend is to be a true friend to someone in need of a friend. To the world you might be only one person, but to one person you might be the world. There are so many people needing a friend. Rather than waiting for someone to come to you to be your friend. Rather than wanting the person whose life is already filled with friends. Rather than wanting the same friend everyone else wants, go and be a friend to someone who needs one.

The Bible says, *"Share each other's burdens"* (Galatians 6:2). This is mutual friendship. Today, find someone who needs you to help them carry their burden. Tomorrow, they will help you carry yours. And maybe even carry you. You've got a friend.

Stephen's Story

THINGS STARTED TO GO BADLY WHEN MY FATHER DIED. I FLEW TO Scotland to attend his funeral. When I arrived at my parents' home, I was startled to see the body being carried out of the house. I was confused as to why the long delay in removing the body from the home. My bewilderment turned to shock when I learned it was my mother's body. Both of my parents were gone. My father from cancer. My mother had committed suicide.

As an only child, I was devastated. I prepared for a double funeral with two caskets at the front of the church. I flew back to Canada and tried to carry on with my life as normal. Unfortunately, things were not normal. I self-medicated and turned to alcohol to deal with the pain and hurt. I woke up one day and had a complete mental breakdown. I became totally psychotic and paranoid. I didn't know where I was. From that point on, I entered a period of serious mental illness. Life was more than I could cope with.

I reached out for help to the medical community. I saw numerous psychiatrists. I was hospitalized in several mental health institutes. When not hospitalized, I would just sleep at home. I basically lay on my couch at home for about ten years between admissions to hospitals. After a while the pain and hurt got so bad that I tried to commit suicide several times. I took overdoses. I cut my wrists. I wasn't sure why I didn't die.

Then one day I seemed to come to my senses. I said to myself, "I don't want to be on this journey any more." I contributed my inability to take my own life to the hand of God. He was preserving my life. He had a purpose for my life. Yes, I had questions. I had become a Christian earlier in my life, so why did my life get to this point? And yet through the fog I had a clear sense that God had never lost sight of me.

Today, I am back to full health with minimal symptoms. My experience has given me compassion, empathy, and an understanding for people who suffer like I did. I work in a community mental health centre, using my experience to help others who suffer from mental illness. I feel the purpose of God living itself out in my life. My greatest fulfillment is seeing my suffering transferred into blessing others.

12 Growing Over the Wall

Years ago, I read a book titled *Beyond the Barriers*. It is the story of a young man named Harold Morris who was sent to prison for a crime he did not commit. Armed robbery. Before he was pardoned, he spent nine and a half years in fear. Each night as he closed his eyes to sleep, he was never sure whether or not he would survive the night. His companions were psychotic killers, rapists, and criminals of all types. He witnessed numerous murders and mutilations. He described the repeated threats on his life, especially after becoming a Christian. Harold began his Christian life already against the wall.

When he was finally released and pardoned, he encountered another wall. A very different kind of wall, but just as deadly. Cancer. Harold Morris wrote,

> We share other adversaries which are the result of a fallen world. Sorrow, tragedy, heartache, insecurity, and loneliness belong to all of us. Financial hardships, broken promises, disintegrating friendships, shattered dreams—they hound us daily. These are just a few of the hurdles we must overcome if we are to finish the race as victorious Christians.[1]

Morris strikes a key truth about life. Experience is a great teacher. We are in a race. A marathon. With lots of hurdles. Obstacles. Walls. Our goal is to finish the race. To be victorious. To get beyond the barriers.

Sometimes we leap over the wall. Sometimes we burrow under. At other times, we make a lateral run around it. But mostly, we grow slowly but surely over the wall.

EVERYTHING IS AGAINST ME

I began this book with the story of Joseph from the book of Genesis. When Joseph's brothers appeared before him needing food, Joseph attempted to discern their hearts. He put them through several hoops before revealing his identity. He tested the welfare of his younger brother Benjamin by holding brother Simeon hostage until they returned to him with Benjamin. The brothers travelled back to Canaan and their father Jacob without Simeon and with the news that Benjamin was to accompany them to Egypt upon their return there. Jacob was devastated and exclaimed, *"Joseph is gone! Simeon is gone! And now you want to take Benjamin, too. Everything is going against me!"* (Genesis 42:36).

That's often how we feel. When we are up against the wall, everything seems against us. Was everything against Jacob? It may have seemed that way. But often things are not what they seem. In fact, everything was about to take a dramatic turn. This was the beginning of one of the most momentous reunion stories in the Bible. Jacob was closer to seeing his son Joseph, again, than he could have possibly believed. For the rest of his life, Jacob would enjoy a reunited family. He would grow older with all of his children and grandchildren around him. Family. Security. Provision. Abundance.

A FRUITFUL TREE

Years later, when father Jacob was dying, he gathered his family around him and spoke to each of them. When it came Joseph's turn, Jacob placed his hand on Joseph's shoulder and said, *"Joseph is a fruitful tree, a fruitful tree beside a spring. His branches reach over the wall"* (Genesis 49:22). His son had become the ruler of Egypt, second only to Pharaoh. Entrusted with a vast famine relief program. Wise. Discerning. Compassionate. The image that came to Jacob's mind was that of a tree growing beside a bubbling spring bearing luscious fruit and reaching up and over the wall.

THE PREREQUISITE FOR FRUIT: PRUNING

A horticulturalist will tell you that for a tree to be fruitful, there are two necessities. The first is pruning. Pruning is essential for fruit-bearing. The pruner takes a knife or scissors and cuts into the tree removing all excess branches and sparing only the branches that promise the best fruit. To the casual observer, pruning appears wasteful. Branches lie strewn everywhere on the ground. If you've ever seen a tree just freshly pruned, it looks more like a horrible haircut under the scissors of a frenzied barber.

When I was a teenager, my father would send his three sons down the street to the village barber. But this was no ordinary barber. He just loved to cut and chop. I would sit in the big leather chair and warn the wiry little man with the big scissors to take off only a little. That meant to remove almost nothing. Hair below the ears and down to the shoulders was the norm. This barber knew nothing about norm. As he started in, I would scowl and grimace just to garner respect for my wishes. He would mumble out little irrational snarls. It was the same routine every time for all three of us belonging to the brotherhood.

The other standard routine was a second visit. I would arrive home to my father's inspection and dissatisfaction. "I thought you went to get a haircut," he would say. "I got one," I would retort. "On what part of the head?" he would ask. On my way back for the second visit, I would meet my brother returning from his first visit. No words were spoken. This was not a happy day. And we knew the routine. I would sit in the chair for the second time and watch in the mirror as the little man cast his spell over my locks with a devilish smirk in the corner of his mouth. At the end of the ordeal, there was more hair on the floor than on the head. I would jump down from the chair of doom and leave without a word of thanks. I would meet my brother on his way in for his customary second visit. Again, no word was spoken. He would just look at me with a certain terrified look. I knew it. This was no haircut; this was a painful pruning. I looked like a tree right after the spring pruning with more branches taken out than left in. I want to say the emotional scars took years to heal, but actually I got over it and moved on with my life.

Jesus taught about the significance of pruning in our lives in John 15:1–2. He said, *"I am the true grapevine, and my Father is the gardener. He cuts off every branch of mine that doesn't produce fruit, and he prunes the branches that do bear fruit so they will produce even more."* God the Father is the Gardener. When God is going to do something wonderful, He often begins with some painful pruning. He uses a pruning knife that cuts deep into your nature. It can leave scars. But note two things. Pruning means God sees fruit in your life and the potential of much more fruit. Pruning is not punishment. It means possibility. Potential. And remember what we learned earlier: pain is the greatest motivator to change. It is necessary if you are to enjoy an increasingly fruitful life. Let the Gardener do His work of pruning. Don't resist it. Don't loathe it. Let it happen.

God saw fruit in the life of the young man Joseph. And He saw more. He saw the potential for this same young man to grow up and play a significant role in God's plan of redemption. But Joseph did not naturally become the man he became. He grew into that man by experiencing the pain of pruning. His dreams were shattered. He hit the wall. He was the target of betrayal and the victim of injustice. Enslaved and imprisoned in a foreign land. Forgotten by everyone except God. But he allowed his God to prune him. His father Jacob acknowledged this at the end of his life when he said of Joseph, *"Archers attacked him savagely; they shot at him and harassed him. But his bow remained taut, and his arms were strengthened by the hands of the Mighty One of Jacob, by the Shepherd, the Rock of Israel"* (Genesis 49:23–24).

WATER SOURCE

The second essential prerequisite for fruit-bearing is a source of life. Water. When Jacob placed his hands on Joseph just before he died, he stated, *"Joseph … is a fruitful tree beside a spring"* (Genesis 49:22). Joseph's source of life, his spring of life-giving water, was the living God within him. Joseph gave personal witness to this truth when he himself acknowledged, *"God intended it all for good. He brought me to this position so I could save the lives of many people"* (Genesis 50:20).

Everything living needs water to survive and bear fruit. I remember the day we travelled down over the Dead Sea escarpment just east of the

Dead Sea. You will have an idea of what it was like if you can visualize breathtaking beauty while at the same time a hot and arid wilderness. There is a deadly absence of water. No evidence of life except snakes, scorpions, and lizards. How could someone possibly survive here? We had just passed a Bedouin camp. How did the Bedouin exist in such a desolate environment? It helped me to understand why the children of Israel complained so much out in the wilderness. It helped me to appreciate the endurance of Moses. Then we spotted something. A lone palm tree growing out of the side of the rocky cliff. I pointed my binoculars in the direction of the tree and saw more foliage and fruit. What did this indicate? There was a source of life. Water. It's called an oasis. I scanned the area with my binoculars and detected some movement higher on the cliff. A steep, narrow path wound its way down the vertical side of the escarpment, and young Bedouin children, pails in hand, were descending to draw water from the spring.

As I have mentioned, one of my interests is to research the lives of the early native peoples and pioneers. And then to go discover and explore where they lived and survived. I just finished exploring the village of Old Washington in the state of Kentucky. This place was the home base of probably the most significant frontiersman in the late 1700s—Simon Kenton. About a mile from the village is the location of Kenton's Station, the site of a blockhouse built by Kenton high on a bluff to provide protection and security for the settlers he welcomed. He built the station in that location because there were two springs. One of them bubbled out of the side of the bluff. I found no marker signifying the location of the spring. All I had was the information I had read. So off I set on my hands and knees through the heavy underbrush below the bluff to see if I could find it. Sure enough, I did. The ground began to feel damp and soggy. Then I heard the sound of bubbling, running water. There it was, coming right out of the side of the bluff, just the way Simon Kenton found it more than two hundred years ago. A spring. A water source was where the early frontier settlers built cabins and settlements. That's where the Indians established their camps and towns. Life needs water.

In this broken world, bad things happen to good people. Tragedy strikes both the good and the bad alike. So what makes the difference?

The source of life. Jesus said, *"Anyone who is thirsty may come to me! Anyone who believes in me may come and drink! For the Scriptures declare, 'Rivers of living water will flow from his heart'"* (John 7:37–38). Jesus understood water to be absolutely necessary for life. And He used the picture of flowing water to represent the life of the Holy Spirit flowing in and through the one who is surrendered to Him. He is our source of life.

In Psalm 1:3, the psalmist spoke about the joy of one who delights in the Scriptures and meditates on them continually. He wrote, *"They are like trees planted along the riverbank, bearing fruit each season."* When you surrender your life to what God says in His Word, the Bible, the roots of your life grow deep into a nonstop flow, a never-ending supply of life-giving water. And the result is fruit.

In John 15:1–2, Jesus said that you need pruning to produce fruit. Then in verse 5, He said you need a source of life to produce fruit. *"I am the vine; you are the branches. Those who remain in me, and I in them, will produce much fruit. For apart from me you can do nothing."* Jesus is the vine. He is the conduit to the water supply. He is the source of life. If you are a believer in Christ, then you are a branch, connected to the vine, to Jesus. In Him, you are connected to the source of life, and you will bear fruit.

THE PRESENCE OF FRUIT

Think of this picture Jesus painted. It is of value to note that the fruit does not hang from the vine. The vine is the source of life. The fruit hangs from the branches. The branches produce fruit because they are in the vine. The presence of fruit in your life is the evidence to those around you of the presence of the living Christ within you.

The presence of fruit in Joseph's life was evident. He had grown up in a home filled with jealousy, favouritism, and hostility. But Joseph was able to break the cycle of hostility in his family of origin. When his brothers anticipated revenge, Joseph forgave. When they expected retribution, Joseph promised to care and provide for them and their families. There is no doubt he had become a fruitful tree. Long before the apostle Paul wrote about the fruit of the Spirit, Joseph gave evidence of it in his life.

CHARACTER

Paul wrote in Galatians 5:22–23, *"The Holy Spirit produces this kind of fruit in our lives: love, joy, peace, patience, kindness, goodness, faithfulness, gentleness, and self-control."* The water source is the life of the Holy Spirit flowing through the vine and into you, the branch. That is why it is called the fruit of the Spirit.

The fruit of the Spirit is in essence the character of Christ. In Romans 8:28, Paul wrote, *"We know that God causes everything to work together for the good of those who love God and are called according to his purpose for them."* It is noteworthy that Joseph assured his anxious and fearful brothers with similar words. *"You intended to harm me, but God intended it all for good"* (Genesis 50:20). Part of that good was the divine purpose of saving the lives of His people. But the other part was the kind of person God had fashioned to fulfill that purpose. The man Joseph. A man who took care of those who had inflicted harm on him. A man who reassured and spoke kindly to the very ones who had betrayed him. A man like Jesus Himself. Paul added that the good which God intends is *"to become like his Son"* (Romans 8:29). God allows you to hit the wall and to endure pain so that He can work good in your life. That good does not necessarily mean everything will work out the way you want. It means that through the pain He cultivates the soil for the growth of fruit in your life. Pain is the richest soil for nurturing fruit. And that fruit is the character of His Son Jesus. To be like Jesus is God's ultimate purpose for your life.

FAITH

There is another primary fruit God is intent on nurturing in your life. Tenacious faith. I talked about faith in more detail in another chapter. But its importance is such that it is worth reviewing. Faith lies at the core of our being as followers of Jesus. Faith is the food and sustenance of hope that tells you to keep going when everything else is telling you to quit. Faith is the voice of confidence that God is bigger than this wall when the voice of reason is saying to give it up. Faith focuses your attention on Him. *"It is impossible to please God without faith"* (Hebrews 11:6). Therefore, it is safe to assume God will do nothing to jeopardize the growth of faith in your life. And He will do whatever it takes to strengthen it.

In James 1:4, James identifies the end product of a person's life as being *"perfect and complete."* He is referring to mature character. Christ-like character. Being like Jesus. Again, this is God's ultimate purpose for your life. But how do you arrive here? James says we do so by growing and cultivating strong endurance (verse 3). We examined this word *endurance* earlier. It is the Greek word *hupomonai*. It is the ability to get up and keep going after being struck down. And how does one grow endurance? Working backwards in what James is saying, endurance is grown when faith is tested (verse 3). And faith is tested and nurtured by trials and trouble (verse 2). Christ-like character, then, begins to develop when storms and struggles test and nurture a tenacious faith. This kind of faith is very important to God and the kind of fruit God wants to see maturing on the branch.

My parents used to live in a small village called Norland, tucked away on the edge of the Haliburton Highlands in Ontario. Their home was just down the road from the home of a man named R. D. Lawrence. R. D. Lawrence was a Canadian naturalist who had lived for many years in the northern Canadian wilderness. He wrote many books about his experiences in the north, but the book that most captivated me was *The North Runner*. It is the story of a relationship that grew between this man and a wolf dog.

Yukon was part wolf and part Alaskan malamute. He became Lawrence's lead sled dog. He was strong, dependable, and had a good sense of direction. One time, they were caught unaware by a sudden, violent snowstorm. When the storm initially swept in, Lawrence drove the dog team as hard as he could in an attempt to reach home. The driving snow began to blur his vision, and the cold wind made him gasp for breath. It didn't take long before the worst happened. They lost the trail. There was no place for suitable shelter, and he feared the storm could continue for many days. Despite his strength and experience in the north woods, his confidence began to fade, and a dreadful sense of panic set in. He could feel the numbing cold gripping his body, and he stood motionless as though hypnotized by the biting wind and whirling snow.

It was then that he felt something nudging him. He looked down and saw the big head of Yukon pushing against him. His eyes were unmistakably communicating that Lawrence was not alone. He was offering his companionship. His eyes were also urging Lawrence to keep moving. He did. He drove the team on into a white nothingness until the wind and cold brought him to the point of exhaustion and collapse. He could no longer control the team. The sentence of death seemed upon him.

All along, Yukon had been balking at the harness, trying to pull the team in another direction. Lawrence had been trying to rein him in. The moment Lawrence became incapable of leading the team, Yukon took command. He veered away from the course on which Lawrence had been driving them and began leading the team on a totally new route. There was no stopping him. He ran with such purpose that Lawrence began to feel a tinge of hope stir within him. Did this dog have some mysterious sense that could enable him to find his way across completely strange terrain and bring them home? In Lawrence's own words,

> I put my trust in him. I thought I might as well make myself as comfortable as possible and husband my energies for whatever might yet lie ahead. I put both feet on the left runner, balanced, swung one leg over the sloping side of the sled, and scrambled onto the platform. Wrapped under the canvas tarpaulin, I waited the outcome of Yukon's leadership.[2]

He got them home.

Faith is not absolving oneself of responsibility. You need to do everything you can do. God has given you strength, ability, diverse resources, and a brain—for a reason. But sometimes you will endure a storm and darkness that is greater than your human resources or experience. The storm seems to carry with it the sentence of death. You hit the wall. God allows you to come to the end of yourself, to the point of helplessness. Why? So you'll learn to depend on Him completely. So you'll let go of the controls. You let Him do what only He can do. You let Him take complete charge. You throw both feet into the sled and rest.

You await the outcome of His leadership. You die to self and allow the life of Christ to live fully in you. To pull you through. That's faith. Tenacious faith. Tough faith. That's fruit that God cultivates and nourishes.

In 2 Corinthians 1:8–10, Paul shared about a time when he hit the wall. *"We were crushed and overwhelmed beyond our ability to endure, and we thought we would never live through it. In fact, we expected to die. But as a result, we stopped relying on ourselves and learned to rely only on God, who raises the dead."* There you have it. Your faith journey slowly brings you to the point where you die to yourself and allow Christ to live His resurrection life in and through you. That's total dependence. Absolute surrender. In 2 Corinthians 4:8–10, Paul expressed it this way:

> *We are pressed on every side by troubles, but we are not crushed. We are perplexed, but not driven to despair. We are hunted down, but never abandoned by God. We get knocked down, but we are not destroyed. Through suffering, our bodies continue to share in the death of Jesus so that the life of Jesus may also be seen in our bodies.*

That's the kind of fruit God wants hanging from the branches of your life. Fruit that gives evidence of the living Christ within you.

Through Paul's words, you begin to recognize that he is speaking about a tough, tenacious faith. Jesus was teaching His disciples a faith lesson when He said, "*If you had faith even as small as a mustard seed, you could say to this mountain, 'Move from here to there,' and it would move. Nothing would be impossible*" (Matthew 17:20). The usual translation compares faith to the size of a mustard seed. The smallness of the mustard seed. Just a little faith can result in extraordinary things. There is nothing wrong with believing in the power of just a small amount of faith.

Joe Amaral, however, shares further insight on the faith of a mustard seed in his book *Understanding Jesus*. He suggests that Jesus is referring to a quality of life in the mustard seed. The mustard plant is a tenacious weed. It grows everywhere. The mustard seed can fall on the hardest, most impenetrable, hostile soil where nothing should grow, and it will take root. The mustard plant is a tough, tenacious plant that can push up through anything. That's the kind of faith Jesus speaks of. A tough, tenacious faith that pushes through every barrier.[3]

Harold Morris, the man whose story I began with in this chapter, wrote about tough faith. You'll recall that he hit two walls. Convicts and cancer.

> I've felt like quitting on God many times. When my fellow prisoners, the guards, and even the parole board wrote off my Christian conversion as being some kind of con game and kept insisting I'd die in prison—sure, I felt like giving up. But I didn't. When doctors said nothing more could be done for my cancer and told me not to get involved in any serious relationship because I probably wouldn't make it—sure, I felt ready to call it quits. But I didn't. Rather, I toughed out the low times in blind faith to my unseen Lord. I'd just get on my knees and ask God to give me the strength I needed for that moment. Not for the whole day, but just for that very moment… … I didn't have all the answers, but I kept believing. I had my doubts, but I kept believing. That's tough faith."[4]

And tough faith, mustard faith, is the fruit of hitting the wall.

THE PURPOSE FOR FRUIT

When father Jacob blessed his son Joseph, he described him as a fruitful tree beside a spring. Then he added, *"His branches reach over the wall"* (Genesis 49:22). That's usually how you conquer walls. You grow over them. Jacob paints a word picture of Joseph's life. A luscious tree, laden with succulent fruit growing over a stone wall.

REPRODUCTION

I can think of two reasons for fruit. Both reasons are given by God when He created the earth. In Genesis 1:11, God said, *"Let the land sprout with … trees that grow seed-bearing fruit. These seeds will then produce the kinds of plants and trees from which they came."* You sink your teeth into a plump peach. It tastes so good that you want to devour the whole thing. Until you get to the centre. You must bite into it carefully because there is something inside hard enough to break a tooth. A seed. And the reason for the fruit. The fleshy fruit surrounds the seed to protect and nourish it. When that same peach seed falls to the ground, it grows another tree—a peach tree. The same kind of tree from which the seed came. The peach tree then bears more fruit—peaches. The reason for fruit is reproduction after its kind.

Now think of it. God allows struggles and pain into your life to grow a certain kind of fruit. Christ-like character and tough faith. Godliness and absolute surrender to God. Pain is the most fertile soil for the growth of this fruit. But this fruit is not an end in itself. It is a means to an end. The purpose is reproduction. The fruit of your life protects and nourishes a seed. It envelops a seed of life, which I would see as the life of Christ within. The fruit is a means to reproducing His life in others. If you are a follower of Christ, then the fruit of your life reproduces after His kind.

This fruit is the legacy you'll leave to your children and grandchildren. It goes far beyond wealth and possessions. It's all about character and faith. Tell them your story. The difficult times. The periods of pain. The struggles. The challenges. The failures. The victories. Tell the story of your faith journey. At the same time, live out your faith. A tough faith. Openly and candidly live like Jesus before them. Let them see Jesus in you. His selfless character. By this you influence and speak into their lives. You reproduce the same fruit and life in the next generation and the next.

Someone has said you can count the number of seeds in an apple. But only God can count the number of apples in a seed. When I think about that, I am reminded that as God grows seed-bearing fruit in my life, only He knows how many fruitful plants and trees will be produced from me after His kind down through the years and generations, long after my fruit tree has died.

ENJOYMENT AND BENEFIT

There's another reason why God gave us fruit. God said, *"I have given you ... all the fruit trees for your food"* (Genesis 1:29). Food. Genesis

2:9 states, *"The* Lord *God made all sorts of trees ... that were beautiful and that produced delicious fruit."* Delicious food. You sink your teeth into a fresh peach. The juice runs down the sides of your mouth. Your taste buds go wild. Your thirst is quenched. You feel refreshed. It tastes delicious. When branches weighed down with fruit reach over the wall, fruit lovers can reach up and pick it. They pull it from the stems and bite into it. It is for their enjoyment and benefit.

Joseph's life produced that kind of fruit. Joseph's life began with a debilitating wall. An incapacitating barrier. But in time, the wall became the path along which the vine matured and grew, until its branches, laden with fruit, reached right over the top and down the other side. Numerous people pulled the luscious fruit from his branches. His family was blessed from the fruit of his life. The people of Egypt were blessed from the fruit of his life. The whole world came to his doorstep and pulled the fruit from his branches. Future generations benefited from the life of Joseph.

God can take a life, no matter how broken against the wall, and produce something of inconceivable value to Himself and others. God will mature and grow the fruit-bearing branches of your life to stretch over the wall so that others can pick from the fruit and find refreshment, enjoyment, and blessing. A young wife and mother, devastated by the sudden death of her husband, works through her grief and begins reaching out to others who are hurting. A young woman gets pregnant and has to drop out of school. When she returns to school, she discovers other young women going through similar struggles and decides to help. A young man is abused by his drunken father all through his growing up years. He always referred to his father as "the old man." But one day the young man falls in love with Jesus, and the Holy Spirit begins to cultivate in him the fruit of love for his father. He is away from home now, but he intentionally calls his father on the phone each week just to say, "I love you, Dad."

Take a moment to insert your own fruit-bearing story at this point.

June was an elderly lady who had encountered some significant walls in her life. Enough heartache and distress to cause severe despondency and emotional breakdown. But Jesus got a hold of June's life. While she would always struggle with her emotional weakness, God gave her new joy and purpose for her life. He gave her a passion for the most vulnerable in our society. She found remarkable fulfillment going into the local nursing home and travelling from bedside to bedside, ministering to the elderly. Listening to the friendless. Holding the hand of the lonely. Brushing the hair of the woman who had forgotten who she was. Speaking life into an old man forsaken by his family and waiting to die.

I will never forget June's seventy-fifth birthday. She sat at home feeling lonely and sorry for herself. Self-pity was dragging her thoughts back into despondency. So she decided to do something about it. She went out and bought the biggest birthday cake she could find. She took it over to the nursing home, cut it up into as many pieces as she could, and served it room to room. Faces lit up. People sang "Happy Birthday." More people celebrated June's seventy-fifth birthday that day than any other birthday in her life. Her loneliness evaporated. Her self-pity was thrust back into its cage. It was the best birthday she had ever had. Why? She was a fruitful tree beside a spring whose branches reached over the wall. The needy reached up and picked the fruit from the branches of her life. They were blessed, and so was she. Oh, yes, she received a birthday card several days later with some money in it. Just the right amount to pay for the cake.

COMFORTING OTHERS

I must add, before I close this chapter, that an essential way to shower the fruit of your life on others is through the ministry of comforting. The word *comfort* means "to infuse with strength." Paul wrote, *"God comforts us in all our troubles so that we can comfort others. When they are troubled, we will be able to give them the same comfort God has given us"* (2 Corinthians 1:4). You hit a wall in your life, and you are broken. Discouraged. Wounded. In some way, the Holy Spirit, either directly or through the Scriptures or through the means of someone else, comes alongside of you and brings comfort. Strength. Healing. Restoration.

But that is not the end. Now you are to be an instrument of the Holy Spirit to carry that same comfort and strength to someone else.

Comforter. Encourager. Counsellor. Helper. These are names given to the Holy Spirit. And now they are fruit cultivated in your life by the Holy Spirit. Fruit that is delicious, enjoyable, refreshing, and needed. Fruit that needs to be shared for the benefit of others.

A DAUGHTER'S NEED

When our daughter Sarah was a little girl and she would scuff her knee or bruise her elbow, she would come running. All I had to do was kiss the bruise and give her a hug. Off she would run. All was fine. When she grew older, it got a little more complicated. In fact, when she entered high school, things got quite convoluted. Things turned upside down for her and for us. She seemed totally unable to cope with school. I found myself spending hours every night helping her with her regular schoolwork. She would cry herself to sleep. At first, we thought it was just a normal adjustment to a new situation. But there was more. Her behaviour was becoming increasingly unmanageable. She developed some obsessive compulsive behaviours. And phobias. She was unable to go into dark, enclosed spaces such as a theatre or subway train. She became afraid of going out anywhere. Afraid of going to sleep. Afraid of dying. She suffered from a severe sleep and anxiety disorder that was getting out of hand. We were getting help from the school, doctors, and counsellors. All to no avail.

The whole situation turned into a most traumatic year for our family. Our peaceful, happy home was filled with tension and strain. Sarah expressed her stress with unruly yelling and unrestrained crying. She understood that she was out of control and even felt extreme guilt over the trauma she was causing. She would often lie in my arms and lament about how awful she was, how sorry she was, and how she hated herself. There was no doubt she had hit a huge, oppressive wall. In fact, our whole family had hit the wall with her. Our soft-natured little girl had changed and seemed to be on a rapid downward spiral.

Quite frankly, Diane and I didn't know what to do. We decided to just ride it out with her and do everything we could to help her and support our other two children through the whole ordeal. We moved her to another school, one where her friends attended, hoping that would help. We continued to get help and support from professionals. We got through the year and things seemed to be settling. The crying and uncontrollable yelling ceased. We seemed to be getting our girl back. However, the sleep and anxiety disorder and some phobias persisted. It concerned us immensely.

Then one day, about five years later, there was a break in the case. It began over a completely different issue. Sarah was feeling remorseful, guilty over something that had happened more recently. But that led to further expression of her feelings of responsibility, remorse, and guilt over the difficult time she felt she had caused for our family several years earlier. It was quite late at night, and we were sitting on the little sofa in the family room. I put my arm around her and said, "We love you more than you will ever know. I just wish that I could get inside your head and understand what is going on and help you."

Tears filled her eyes. She looked at me and said, "Dad, you wouldn't understand. I'm so bad, and you're so good. I respect you more than anyone I know. It's like you're perfect. I don't think that you would identify." I felt my heart begin to bleed. As it bled, it began to speak. I held her tightly and asked if I could tell her my story. She nodded. I cherished her respect and admiration. But she also needed to know the real me. With vulnerability and transparency and recognizable risk, I shared my story with her. I verbalized in detail the walls I had hit in my life. My failures. Defeats. Deficiencies. Struggles. I shared where God's restorative grace had been so powerful in my life. I shared the ways God had comforted and encouraged me.

As I spoke, it was like God was using me to comfort Sarah with the same comfort with which He had comforted me. It was like God was lifting a weight from her heart. I also had been in the place of need. I also had been in the place of weakness. God had spoken strength into my life. Now, I was speaking strength into her life. She was picking fruit from the branches of my life.

As time went on, the healing process opened up the old wounds of that earlier painful episode. A series of events and some vivid flashbacks revealed that that chapter of her life had been triggered by something that had happened inside our own home. Something that shocked and disturbed me deeply. A trusted visitor had sexually assaulted her at night in her own bedroom while she slept. He had crept into her room on several occasions. I felt overwhelmed. Angry. Devastated. But what Sarah needed was comfort. Again, my desire was that Sarah be able to reach up and pull the fruit of comfort, strength, and wisdom from the branches of my life. Branches and fruit that had grown over the wall in my own life from which she would now benefit, grow, and mature. There were others who played a vital role in her healing. Her mother. Brother. Sister. And when she married, a very understanding husband. God brought a special doctor into her life. This particular doctor had hit some sizeable walls in his own life. He knew the trauma of emotional pain from personal experience. Sarah was able to pick the fruit from the branches of his life and benefit immensely. It took all of us.

We got our daughter back. The disorders and phobias disappeared. Sarah has grown into a godly and mature woman. She lives with a strong sense of purpose and has a healthy emotional well-being. The Holy Spirit has cultivated and nourished the rich fruit of strength, compassion, wisdom, discernment, faith, and Christ-like character on the branches of her life. Those fruit-laden branches reach over her wall. And I am certain that for the rest of her life, others will benefit and be blessed from picking the fruit of those branches.

May your fruitful branches grow over the wall. No wall is too high. May others in need of restoration and nourishment find enjoyment, healing, and blessing as they reach up and partake of the fruit of your life.

Memory Aids

Memory is a wonderful gift. It connects the dots of your life. It connects us to one another, to familiar places, to where we have come from, to our past. It connects us to what God has done. God wants us to keep our memory green. Alive. He wants us to remember the circumstances of the past, not to be controlled negatively by them, but to be propelled positively and steered forward by them. Memories of the past should not be like an anchor dragging all kinds of debris along with you as you slowly struggle forward. But more like a rudder behind the ship of your life giving direction, guidance, and inspiration as you progress forward.

The Israelites had wandered in the desert for forty years. Finally, they were on the verge of moving into Canaan, the land God had promised them. The anticipation was intense. Except for one little problem. Well, not so little. The Jordan River was in the way. And there was no Allenby Bridge waiting for them. Now what?

You can read the whole story in Joshua 3. Joshua followed God's instructions to the letter. When the priests' feet touched the water at the river's edge, God cut the flow of water off upstream. That was something only God could do. That's supernatural. That's a miracle. Then the people, all several million of them, began to move in an orderly but intentional manner across the dry ground. When everyone was safely across, God instructed that twelve men pick up one stone each from the middle of the riverbed and carry these stones on their shoulders to the place where they would be camped that night. They were to use these stones to construct a memorial there. This was done.

Before God released the water, Joshua looked back across the dry riverbed and was speechless at what had just occurred. What an amazing God! He returned to the middle of the riverbed where the priests were still standing with the Ark of the Lord's Covenant resting on their shoulders. (You have to empathize with the priests, who had been standing there all day. Their feet and shoulders must have been killing them. You can only hope they had a shift system in place.) Joshua picked up twelve more of the biggest stones he could find and lift. He piled them as high as he could. He then turned to the priests and commanded, "Let's go!"

As soon as the last sandal sole lifted from the riverbed, so did the hand of God lift from the waters upstream. Immediately, like an exploding dam, the water cascaded down along the dry waterway, overflowing the banks once again. When the water had returned to its seasonal levels, the river rolled along as normal, as though nothing had happened. But something incredible had taken place. There was nothing normal. And something told the story. Some stones could be seen projecting above the surface of the water out in the middle of the river.

Two piles of stones—one at the first encampment and one in the middle of the Jordan River. Why? Joshua gave the reason in Joshua 4:21–24.

> *In the future your children will ask, "What do these stones mean?" Then you can tell them, "This is where the Israelites crossed the Jordan on dry ground." For the* LORD *your God dried up the river right before your eyes, and he kept it dry until you were all across, just as he did at the Red Sea … He did this so all the nations of the earth might know that the* LORD*'s hand is powerful, and so you might fear the* LORD *your God forever.*

The stones stood lest the people forget what God had done. This was a place where God did something astonishing. This was a place where God manifested His supernatural power. This was also the always-sunny, dry Jericho tourist region where, for generations, parents would bring their children on vacation. When their children looked out at the Jordan River near where it flowed into the Dead Sea, they would see some stones standing out of the water in the middle of the river. They would naturally ask, "What is that? How did those stones get out there?" The parent would then respond, "Let me tell you what God did."

Diane and I are strong advocates of memory aids. We fill our home with them. I fill my office with them. God is a strong believer in memory aids. He has filled His Word with the record of them.

He set a rainbow in the sky as a reminder of His promise never to destroy the world again with water.

Altars were often used as memory aids. An altar was to be constructed of earth or natural uncut stones. It was a simple place of worship, sacrifice, and remembrance. Everywhere Abraham went, he built an altar as a reminder of God's presence and promises. After the victory God gave to the Israelites over the Amalekites, Moses built an altar and named it "the Lord is my Banner." It was a reminder of how we move under the banner of the Lord and He is our victory.

Stones were a common memory aid. On the first night of Jacob's flight from home, he was so tired that he laid his head on a stone and fell fast asleep. He had hit a major wall in his life. That night, Jacob had a dream of a ladder reaching up into heaven and God reassuring him of His presence and protection. The next morning, Jacob realized he had encountered the living God. He had been in God's presence. He set his stone pillow upright as a memorial pillar to remind him of this divine encounter. He named the place Bethel, meaning "house of God." God gave the Israelites a miraculous victory over the Philistines. Samuel took a large stone and set it on its end. He named it Ebenezer, meaning "the stone of help," a reminder that God had helped them and stands ready to help you in your time of need. When passersby saw that stone out in the field and asked its meaning, one would reply, "Let me tell you what God did."

The feast days of ancient Israel pointed back to the redemptive work of God and forward to Christ. The Sabbath day reminded the observer of the marvelous Creator and of the God who had redeemed and liberated the Israelites from slavery in Egypt and brought them out with a strong hand and powerful arm (Deuteronomy 5:12–15). Israelites wore tassels on the hem of their clothing attached with a blue cord as a reminder to obey all of God's commands and to live holy lives. I have a Jewish friend who wears four tassels from his shirt to remind him of God's commands and the need to obey Him. A two-quart jar of manna was placed in the tabernacle as a reminder of God's miraculous, faithful provision during their forty years in the wilderness.

Jesus Himself gave us the wonderful memory aids of the bread and wine as reminders of His body broken and His blood shed for us. I guess He knows how prone we are to forget. The bread and cup are opportunities for us to say, "Let me tell you what Jesus did."

Even physical scars can be memory aids. You remember the night Jacob fought with God at the Jabbok River. He encountered God face to face and did not know it until daybreak. That was when the divine wrestler only touched Jacob's hip, and Jacob dropped to the dust. Ever after, Jacob walked with a limp. Every time Jacob got up and walked, he was reminded of the time God broke him, of the place of surrender. Whenever someone curiously asked Jacob why he walked with a limp, he could reply, "Let me tell you what God did."

The apostle Paul suffered a physical affliction. He called it a *"thorn in my flesh"* (2 Corinthians 12:7). He prayed that God would remove it, but God said no. Paul was to wear the ailment as a reminder of God's grace and strength in his weakness. Physical and emotional scars can be memory aids that take you back to a time when you struggled at the wall. A place where you discovered God's grace and strength in a whole new way. A place of brokenness and humble surrender. Something God did in your life.

I have already shared with you about some of our personal memory aids. Photos tell a story of change and of God's faithfulness and provision through the changing years. Our "fleece" photos are a reminder of God's leading. I don't wear tassels, but I wear a black wristband that says, "God is strong." I often have strangers ask me what the wristband means, and I have a great opportunity to tell them that it is a reminder to me that God is the strength of my life. We have a "memory wall" in our home. Framed pictures of the homes we have lived in hang on the memory wall. They tell our family the story of God's involvement and provision through the years. While we have moved from the home we called "Our Bethesda," we have the signboard that hung on a post at the end of our driveway now hanging on a wall in our present home as a memory aid that the Lord is our place of healing. I have mentioned the small cottage-like home in our town where we lived for three months. Every time we drive by it, it stands out as a memory aid of God's perfect timing and wonderful provision. All of these are memory aids that remind us of what God has done.

I have a grouse mounted on the wall in my office. It is a reminder that we progress on our knees in prayer. I came upon it in the snow one winter. Our small church had purchased a piece of property on which we planned to erect a facility one day. But there were significant challenges. So I committed myself to walking and praying on the property every Tuesday morning, claiming it for God's purposes. On this particular morning, a snowstorm had blown in about three feet of snow the night before. I tried to convince God that this was not a good morning for my prayer walk. Too much snow for easy walking. But He would not give me a settled feeling about neglecting it that morning. So off I trekked through the snow. That's when I spotted it. A small mound in the snow. I nudged it and recognized the frozen grouse. The beautiful bird, adorned in camouflaged feathers, had probably struck a branch in the night as it flew through the thick pine brushwood, knocked itself out, and frozen. Diane came up with the suggestion that, because of what I was doing when I uncovered it, I have it mounted and placed in a significant spot as a reminder that God answered my prayer. And so, the grouse is perched over my desk. Another memory aid that God hears us when we call. Many times I have been asked the meaning of the bird, and I have had an opening to say, "Let me tell you what God has done."

I have a stack of encouragement cards and letters I've received from people over the years. Memory stones that remind me of how God has used me in some small way in another's life. It leads me to humble gratitude. I have other kinds of letters as well: hostile, inflammatory, and accusatory. These are reminders of God's grace, protection, and faithfulness through some pretty difficult times.

It is important to remember those tough times when you hit the wall. Those crucial turning points in your life. Memory aids help you to remember. A particular rock in your garden can be your Ebenezer, your "stone of help," taking you back to a specific time when the Lord helped you. The God who was with you then is with you today and will be with you tomorrow.

Memory aids tell the story of your spiritual encounters with God. They tell your personal story of God's provision in your times of need. They are an *aide memoire* of how God uses walls to toughen faith, grow endurance, and cultivate character. They point to God's power and promises in your life. They are reminders of the lessons that are, more often than not, learned at the wall. The kinds of lessons Paul learned at his wall of physical ailment. That the wall is the place of humble surrender. God's grace is always sufficient for your need. God's strength is perfected in your weakness.

Your life is the most significant memory aid that you possess. It is the living evidence of the power of God to change and transform a human life. You are the evidence of what only God can do in a life at the wall, the place of pain, the place of brokenness, the place of surrender, the place of transformation. Your life is what you can point to and say, "Let me tell you what God has done."

Endnotes

INTRODUCTION

1. Michael Lewis, *The Blind Side: Evolution of a Game* (New York: W.W. Norton & Company, 2007), 311.

2. Andrew Culverwell, "Cover Me," *My Prayer for You.* Audiocassette. (Word Records Ltd., 1984).

CHAPTER ONE

1. Paul Brand and Philip Yancey, *In His Image* (Grand Rapids: Zondervan Publishing House, 1984), 228.

2. Brand and Yancey, *In His Image*, 241.

3. Elie Wiesel, *Night* (New York: Bantam Books, 1960), 31.

4. Wiesel, *Night*, 62.

5. Ibid., 73.

6. Pamela Reeve, *Faith Is...* (Portland Oregon: Multnoma Publishing, 1970, 1973).

7. William Lane, *The Gospel According to Mark* (Grand Rapids: Eerdmans, 1974), 573.

CHAPTER TWO

1. Dean Merrill, *Another Chance: How God Overrides Our Big Mistakes* (Grand Rapids: Zondervan Publishing House, 1981), 55.

2. John Hiscock, "I've Done Things I'm Not Proud Of," *The National*, "Saturday Magazine," March 13, 2010: 21.

3. St. John of the Cross, *Dark Night of the Soul*, translated by E. Allison Peers (New York: Image, Doubleday Publishing, 1959), 106.

4. J. I. Packer, *Knowing God* (London: Hodder and Stoughton, 1973), 274–275.

CHAPTER THREE

1. Erwin Lutzer, *Failure: The Back Door to Success* (Chicago: Moody Press, 1975), 17.

2. Merrill, *Another Chance*, 17.

3. Ibid., 109.

4. Lutzer, *Failure: The Back Door to Success*, 53.

5. Stanley W. Green, *The Canadian Mennonite* (Sept. 4, 2000), quoted in *Leadership* (Spring, 2001), 71.

6. Craig Groeschel, *It: How Churches and Leaders and Get It and Keep It* (Grand Rapids: Zondervan Publishing House, 2008), 111.

7. Groeschel, *It*, 114.

CHAPTER FOUR

1. David A. Seamands, *Healing for Damaged Emotions* (Wheaton: Victor Books, 1981), 12.

2. Peter Scazzero, *Emotionally Healthy Spirituality* (Nashville: Integrity Publishers, 2006), 109–110.

3. Chris Carrier, http://www.baptiststandard.com/2001/11_26/pages/carrier.html.

CHAPTER FIVE

1. St. John of the Cross, *Dark Night of the Soul*, 106.

2. Scazzero, *Emotionally Healthy Spirituality*, 122–123.

3. Scazzero, 129.

4. Bill Hybels, *The God You're Looking For* (Nashville: Thomas Nelson Publishers, 1997), 21, 22.

5. Eugene H. Peterson, *Leap Over a Wall* (New York: Harper Collins Publishers, 1997), 79.

6. A. W. Tozer, *The Knowledge of the Holy* (New York: Harper and Row, Publishers, 1961), 115.

CHAPTER SIX

1. Grant Jeffrey, *Creation: Remarkable Evidence of God's Design* (Toronto: Frontier Research Publications, Inc., 2003), 246.

2. Groeschel, *It*, 95.

3. Ibid.

4. Mark Driscoll, *Vintage Church* (Wheaton: Crossway Books, 2008), 305.

CHAPTER SEVEN

1. Source Unknown.

2. Bruce E. Olson, *Bruchko* (Altamonte Springs, FL: Creation House, 1973), 144.

3. Olson, *Bruchko*, 144.

4. Henri M. J. Nouwen, *Sabbatical Journey: The Diary of His Final Year* (New York: Crossroad Publishing, 1998), viii.

5. Nouwen, *Sabbatical Journey*, viii.

CHAPTER EIGHT

1. John Ingles Sr., as edited by Roberta Ingles Steele and Andrew Lewis Ingles, *Escape from Indian Captivity* (Radford, VA, 1969), 11, 12.

2. Ibid., 13.

3. http://www.winstonchurchill.org/learn/speeches/speeches-of-winston-churchill/128-we-shall-fight-on-the-beaches.

4. http://www.winstonchurchill.org/learn/speeches/speeches-of-winston-churchill/122-their-finest-hour.

CHAPTER NINE

1. Steve Fisher, *On the Bright Side of Life* (The Costco Connection, May/June 2009), 24.

2. Michael J. Fox, *Always Looking Up: The Adventures of an Incurable Optimist* (New York: Hyperion, 2009), 6.

3. William J. Patterson, *Soldiers of the Queen* (The Canadian Grenadier Guards Corporation, 2009), 270.

4. Ibid., 272.

CHAPTER TEN

1. Geron Davis, "Holy Ground," *Hosanna Music: Come & Worship* (Mobile: Integrity Music, Inc., 1994), 65.

CHAPTER ELEVEN

1. Kevin Belmonte, *William Wilberforce: A Hero for Humanity* (Grand Rapids: Zondervan, 2007), 137–138.

2. Ann Spangler, Lois Tverberg, *Sitting at the Feet of Rabbi Jesus* (Grand Rapids: Zondervan, 2009), 74.

3. Carole King, as performed by James Taylor. "You've Got a Friend," Colgems EMI Music (ASCAP), 1971.

4. Allan W. Eckert, *The Frontiersmen* (Ashland: Jesse Stuart Foundation, 2001), 430.

5. Eckert, *The Frontiersmen*, 414.

6. *Gladiator.* Dir. Ridley Scott. Perf. Russell Crowe. (Red Wagon Entertainment, Scott Free Productions, 2000).

7. Ibid.

8. Ibid.

CHAPTER TWELVE

1. Harold Morris, *Beyond the Barriers* (Pomona: Focus on the Family Publishing, 1987), viii.

2. R. D. Lawrence, *The North Runner* (New York: Ballantine Books, 1979), 112.

3. Joe Amaral, *Understanding Jesus* (Milton: Almond Publications, 2009), 79–80.

4. Morris, *Beyond the Barriers*, ix, x.